The 8th Garfield Treasury

The 8th Garfield Treasury

BY: JIM DAVIS

BALLANTINE BOOKS • NEW YORK

A Ballantine Book
Published by The Random House Publishing Group

The Sunday strips appearing here in color were previously in black and white in
GARFIELD HITS THE BIG TIME #25, GARFIELD PULLS HIS WEIGHT #26,
GARFIELD DISHES IT OUT #27, and GARFIELD LIFE IN THE FAT LANE #28.

Published in the United States by Ballantine Books,
an imprint of The Random House Publishing Group,
a division of Random House, Inc., New York, and simultaneously
in Canada by Random House of Canada Limited, Toronto.

www.ballantinebooks.com

Library of Congress Catalog Card Number: 95-94224

ISBN: 978-0-345-39778-2

First Edition: November 1995

19 18 17 16 15 14 13

The 8th Garfield Treasury

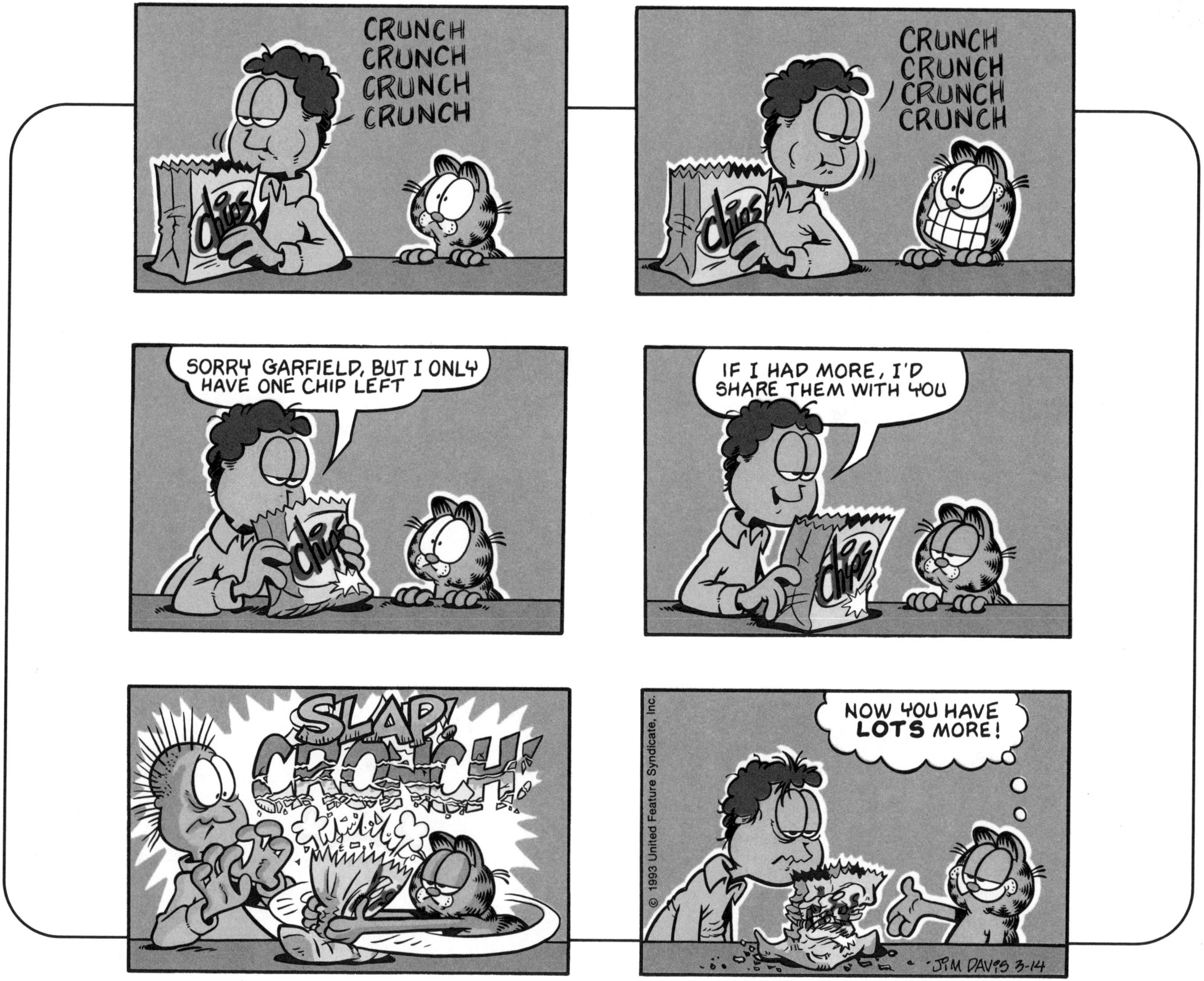
CRUNCH
CRUNCH
CRUNCH
CRUNCH
chips
CRUNCH
CRUNCH
CRUNCH
CRUNCH
chips
SORRY GARFIELD, BUT I ONLY HAVE ONE CHIP LEFT
chips
IF I HAD MORE, I'D SHARE THEM WITH YOU
chips
SLAP!
CRUNCH!
NOW YOU HAVE LOTS MORE!
© 1993 United Feature Syndicate, Inc.
JIM DAVIS 3-14

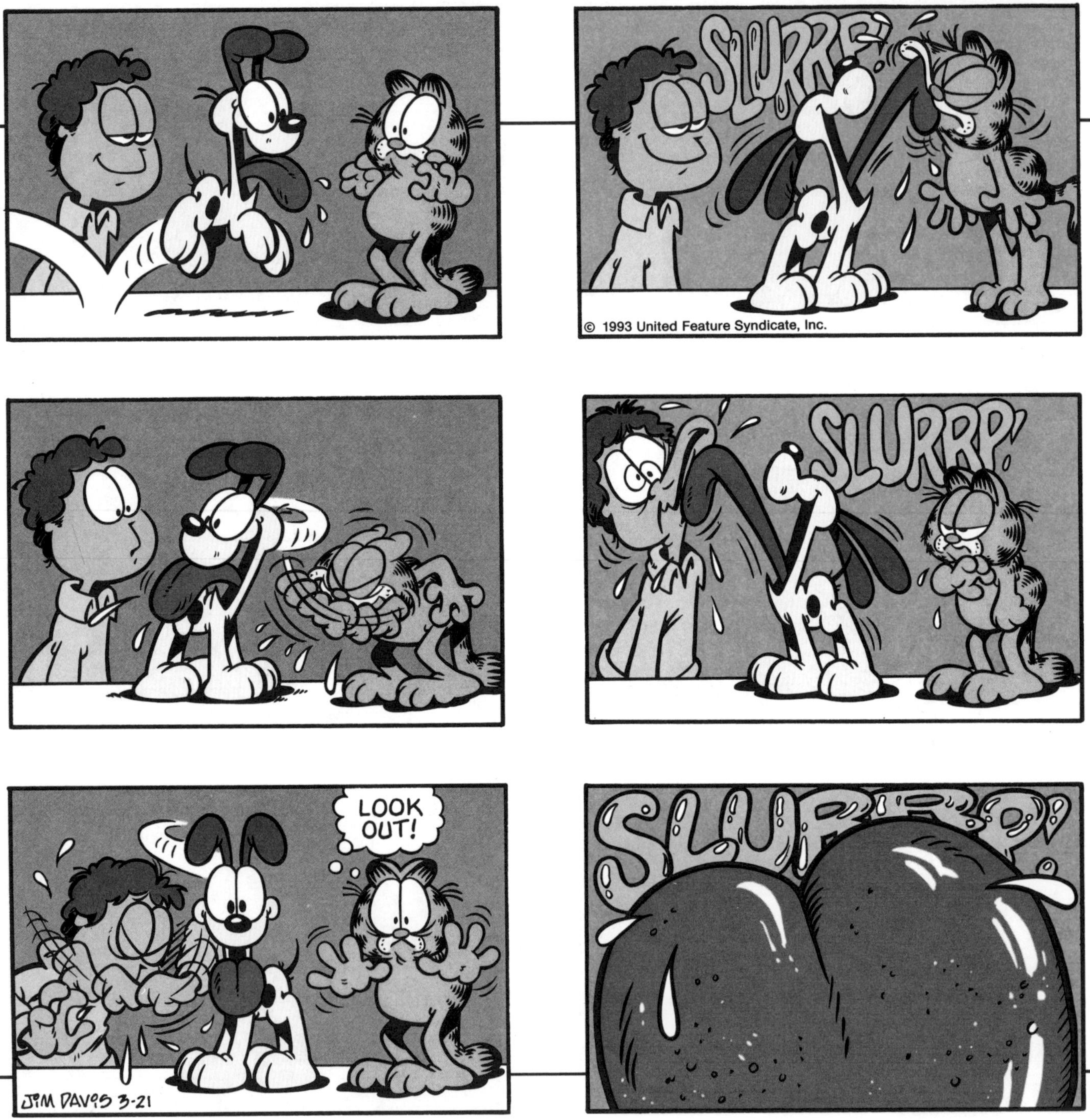
JIM DAVIS 3-21
LOOK OUT!
SLURRP!
© 1993 United Feature Syndicate, Inc.
SLURRP!

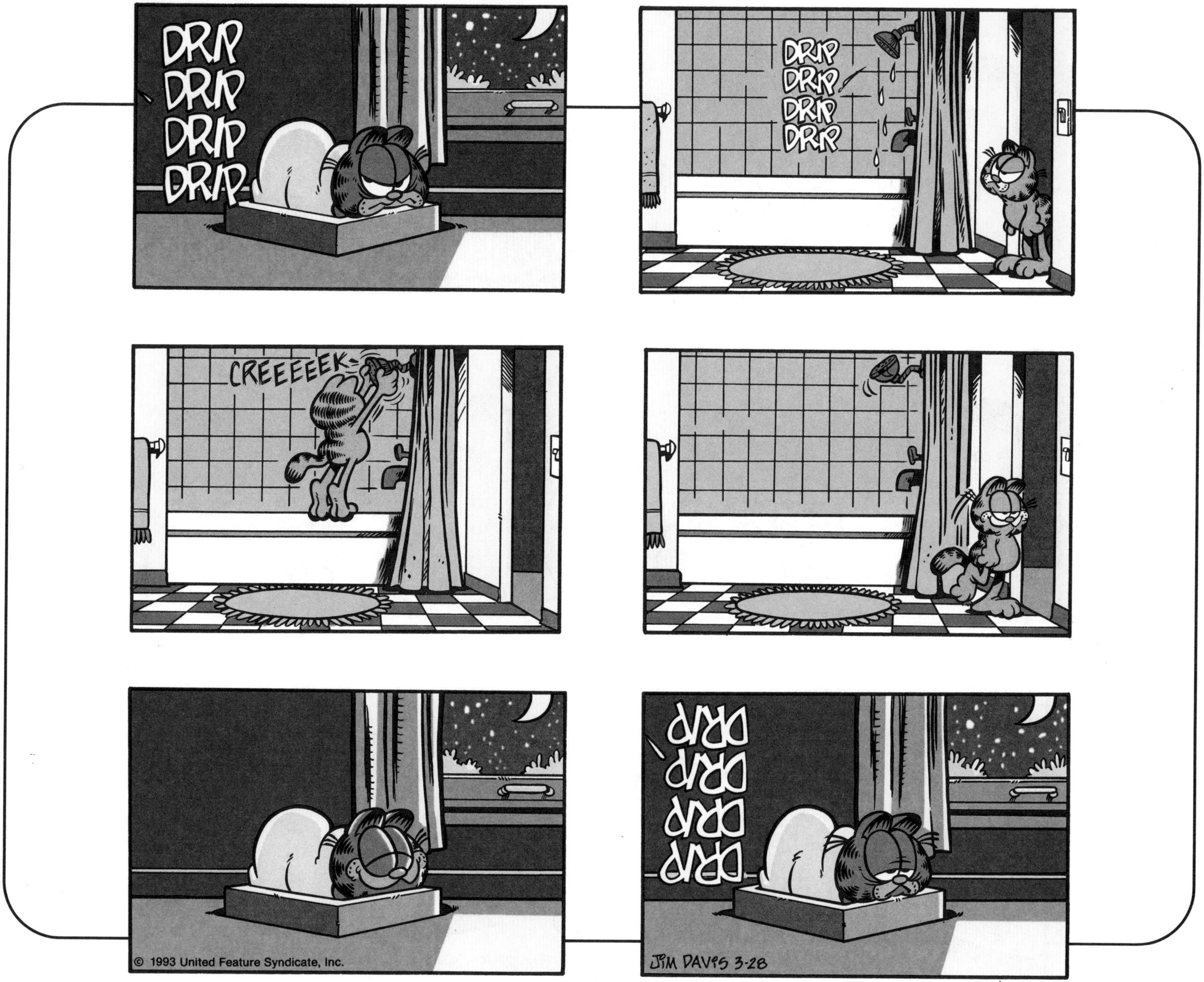
DRIP
DRIP
DRIP
DRIP
DRIP
DRIP
DRIP
DRIP
CREEEEEK
DRIP
DRIP
DRIP
© 1993 United Feature Syndicate, Inc.
JIM DAVIS 3-28

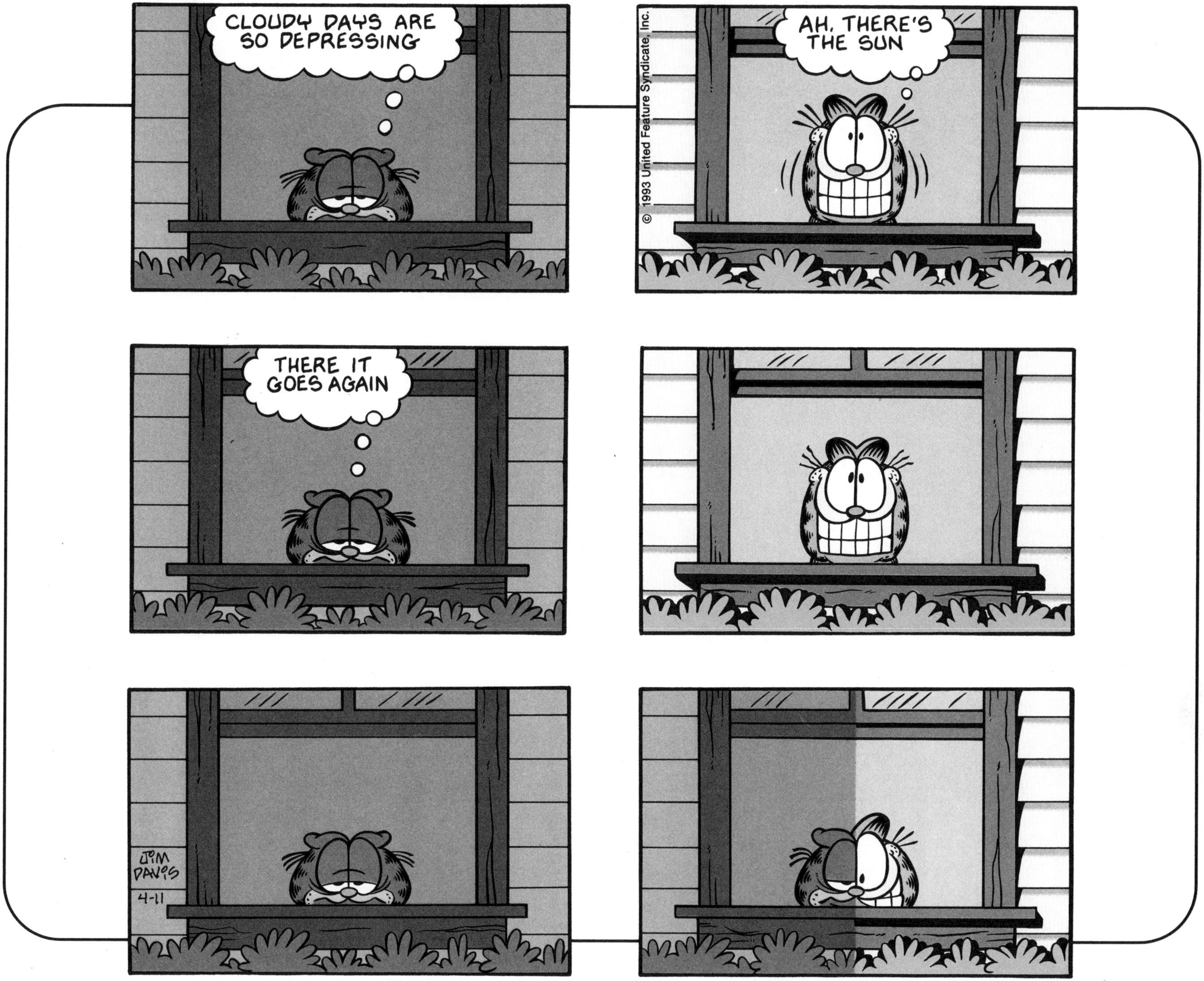
CLOUDY DAYS ARE SO DEPRESSING
AH, THERE'S THE SUN
THERE IT GOES AGAIN
© 1993 United Feature Syndicate, Inc.
JIM DAVIS 4-11

JIM
DAVIS

4-25

SIGH

DOESN'T IT BUG YOU WHEN DOGS GET IN FRONT OF YOU JUST BECAUSE THEY WANT YOUR

ATTENTION

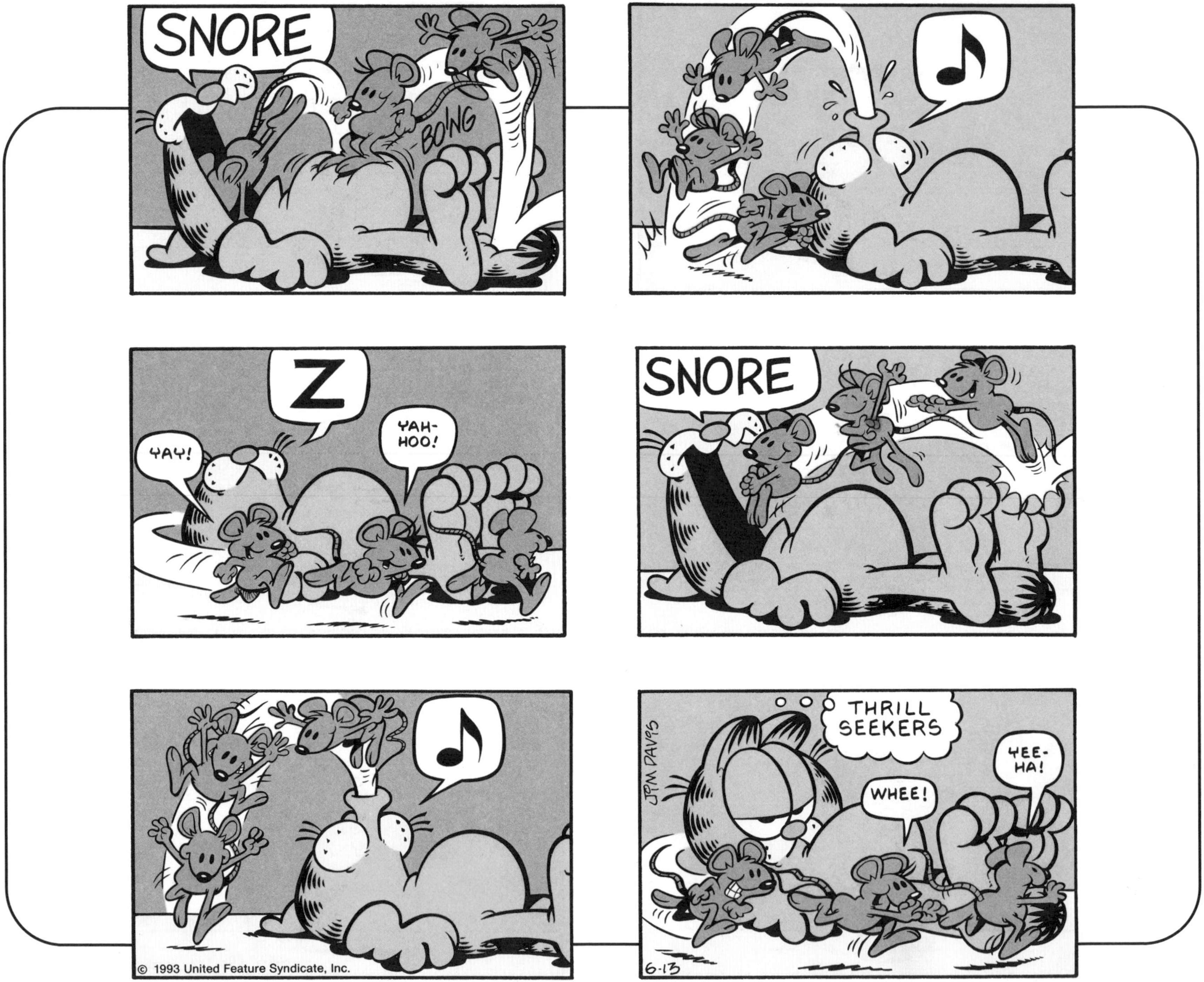
SNORE
BOING
Z
YAY!
YAH-HOO!
SNORE
THRILL SEEKERS
WHEE!
YEE-HA!
JIM DAVIS
6-13

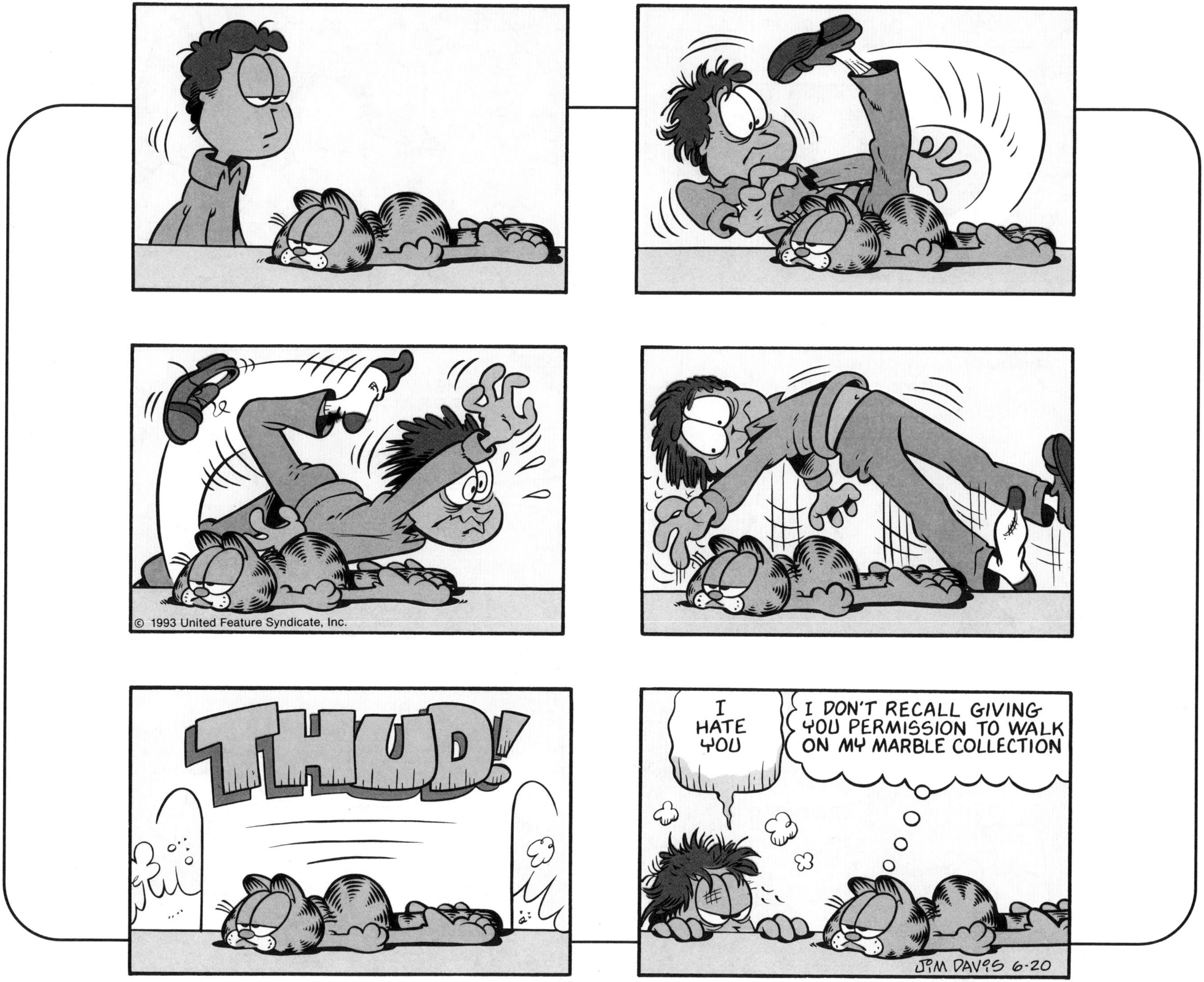

© 1993 United Feature Syndicate, Inc.
THUD!
I HATE YOU
I DON'T RECALL GIVING YOU PERMISSION TO WALK ON MY MARBLE COLLECTION
JIM DAVIS 6-20

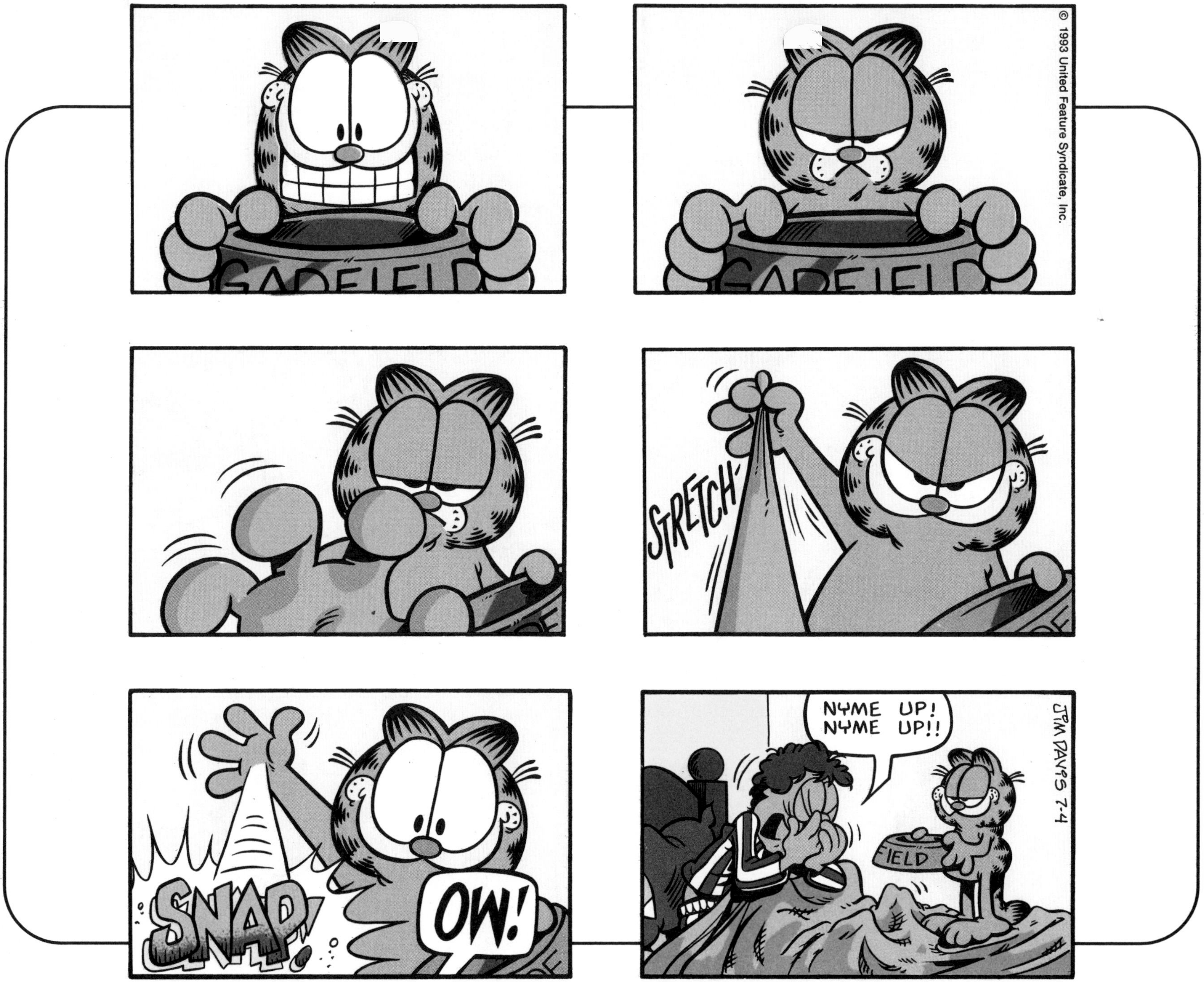

© 1993 United Feature Syndicate, Inc.
STRETCH
SNAP
OW!
NYME UP!
NYME UP!!
JIM DAVIS 7-4

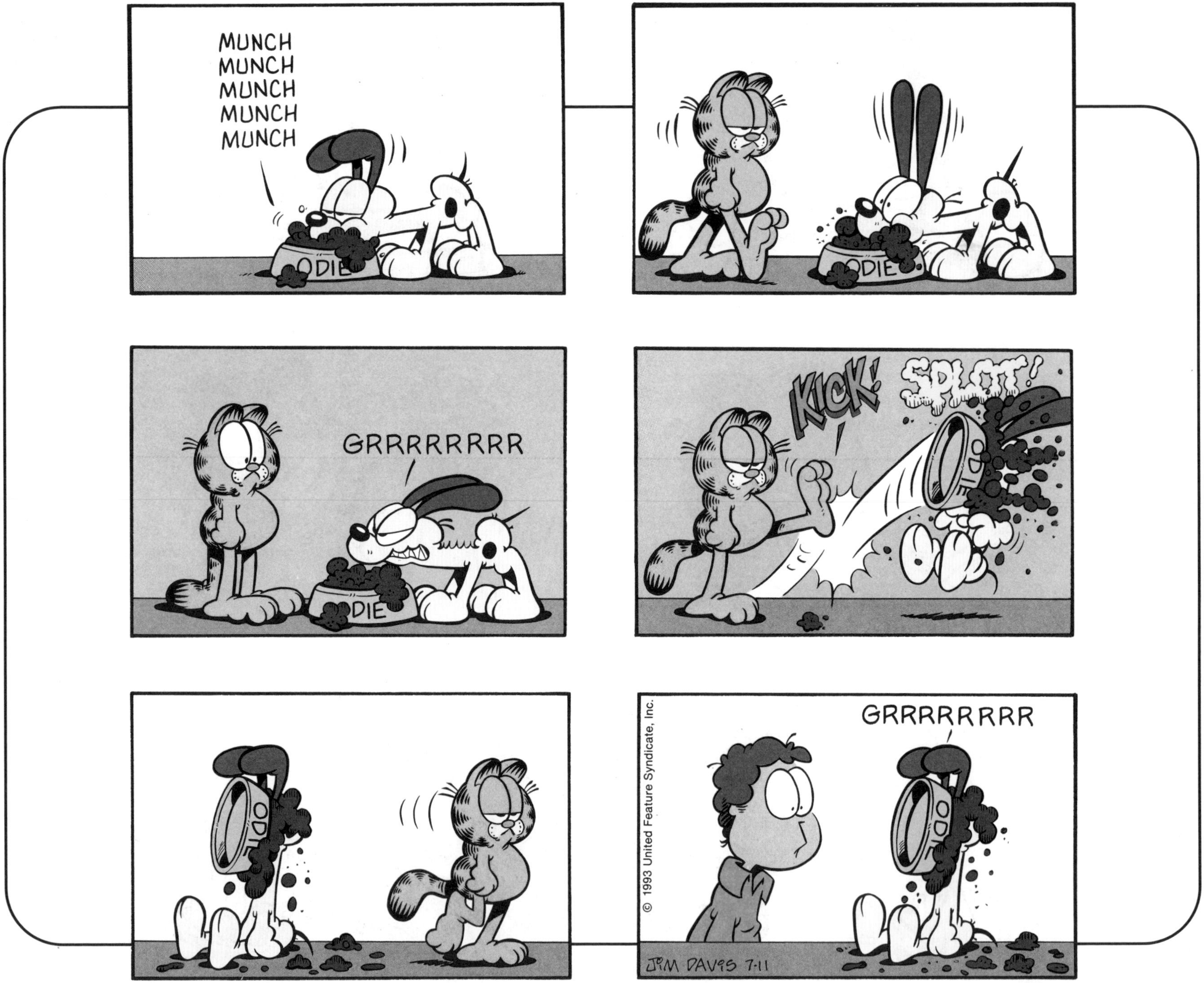
MUNCH
MUNCH
MUNCH
MUNCH
MUNCH
ODIE
ODIE
GRRRRRRRR
ODIE
KICK!
SPLOT!
ODI
ODI
© 1993 United Feature Syndicate, Inc.
GRRRRRRRR
ODI
JIM DAVIS 7-11

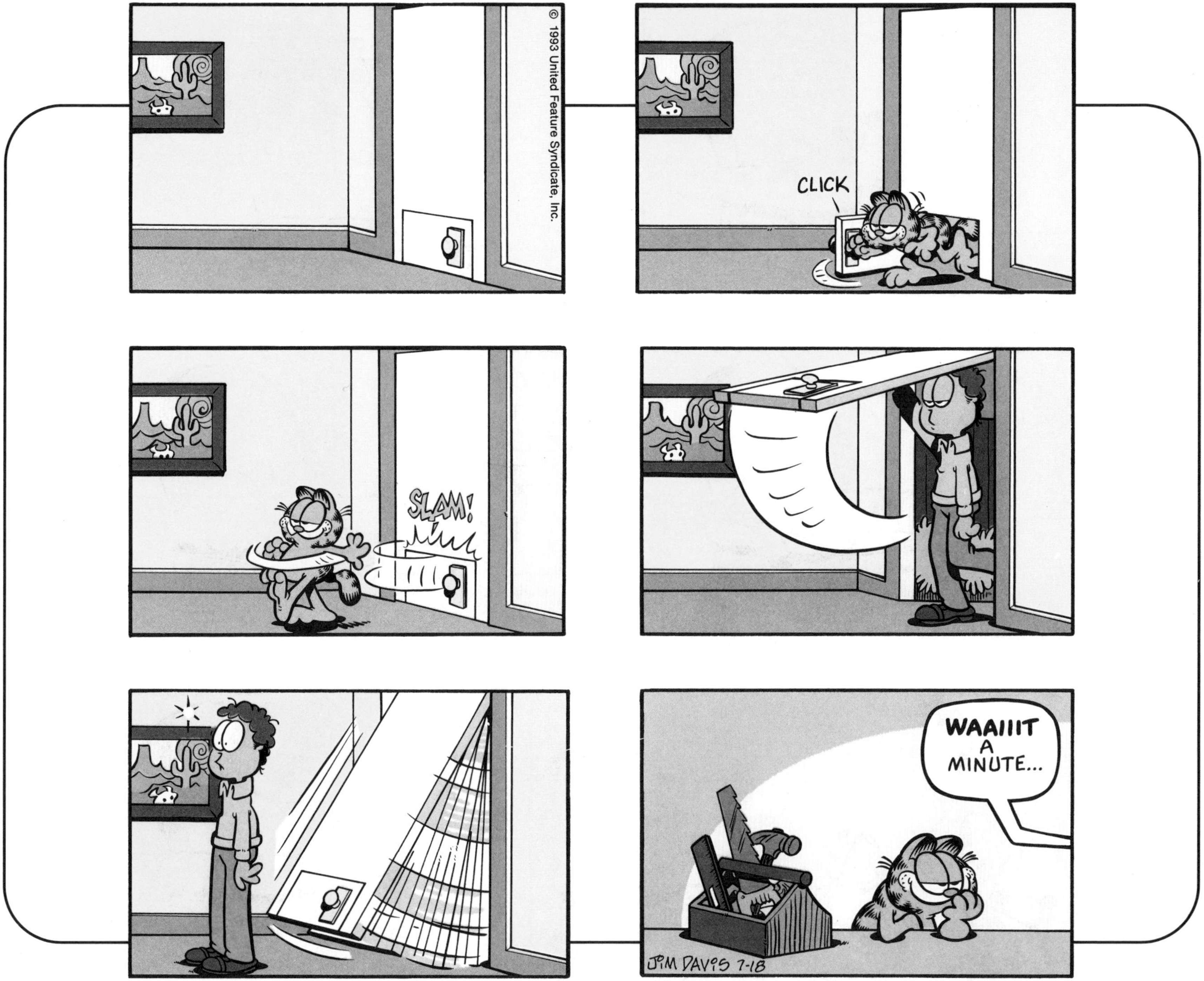
© 1993 United Feature Syndicate, Inc.
CLICK
SLAM!
WAAIIIT A MINUTE...
JIM DAVIS 7-18

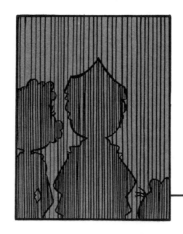

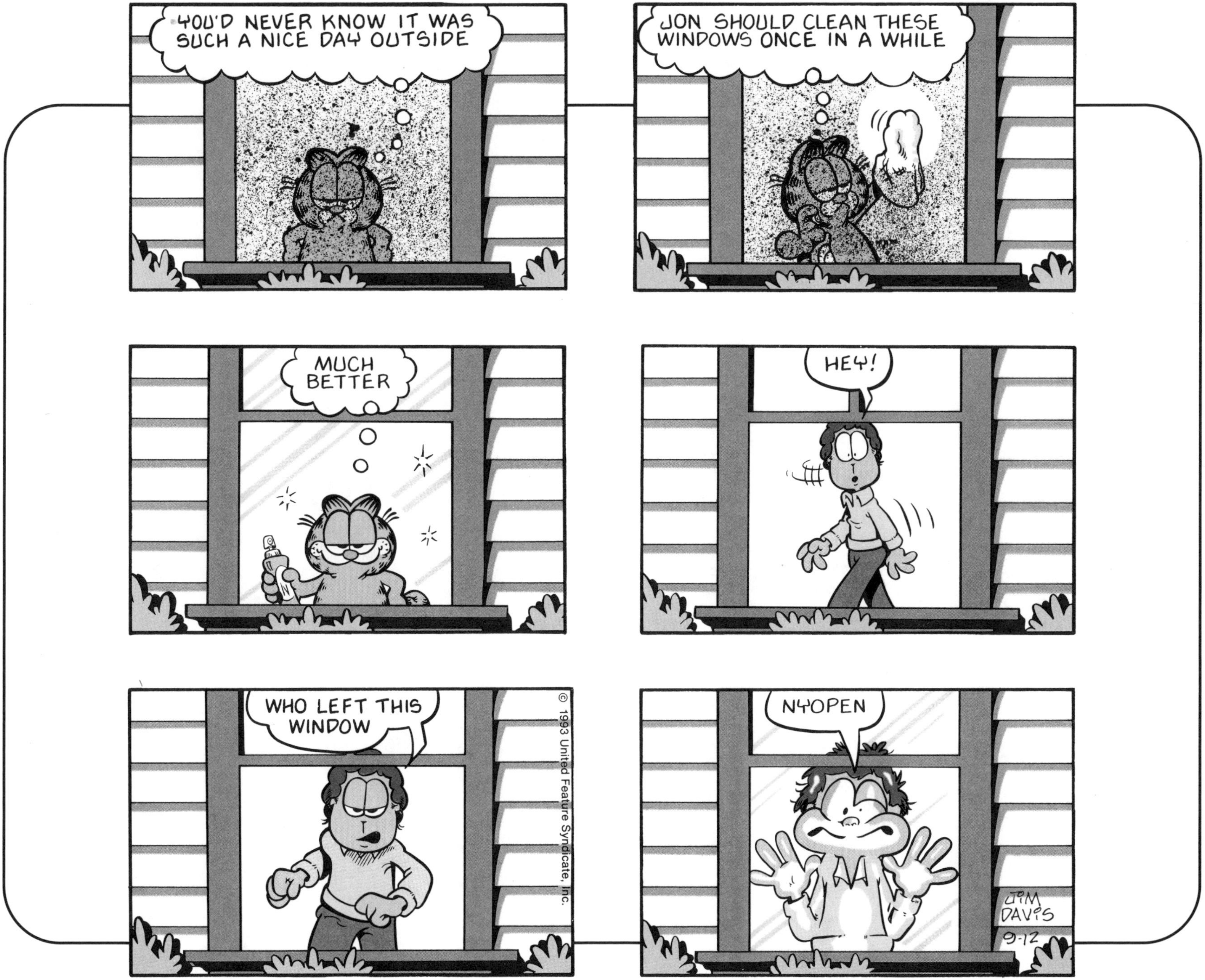
YOU'D NEVER KNOW IT WAS SUCH A NICE DAY OUTSIDE
JON SHOULD CLEAN THESE WINDOWS ONCE IN A WHILE
MUCH BETTER
HEY!
WHO LEFT THIS WINDOW
NYOPEN
JIM DAVIS 9-12

"WILLARD NORF... LOST HIS FRONT TEETH WHEN HE GOT HIS POCKET PROTECTOR CAUGHT IN A GRAIN THRESHER"

"SIDNEY WASSLE... OWNER OF THE WORLD'S LARGEST COLLECTION OF EARWAX"

"MARVIN SMALTZ... ACCIDENTALLY GLUED HIS FINGER UP HIS NOSE"

9·19

"MURRAY KRAVITZ... NEVER WENT TO THE BEACH WITHOUT WEARING SNOW PANTS"

"MYRNA FEEN... FIVE-TIME WINNER OF THE MS. ZIT COMPETITION"

© 1993 United Feature Syndicate, Inc.

GARFIELD, WE'RE WALKING ON HALLOWED GROUND

THE NERD HALL OF FAME

JIM DAVIS

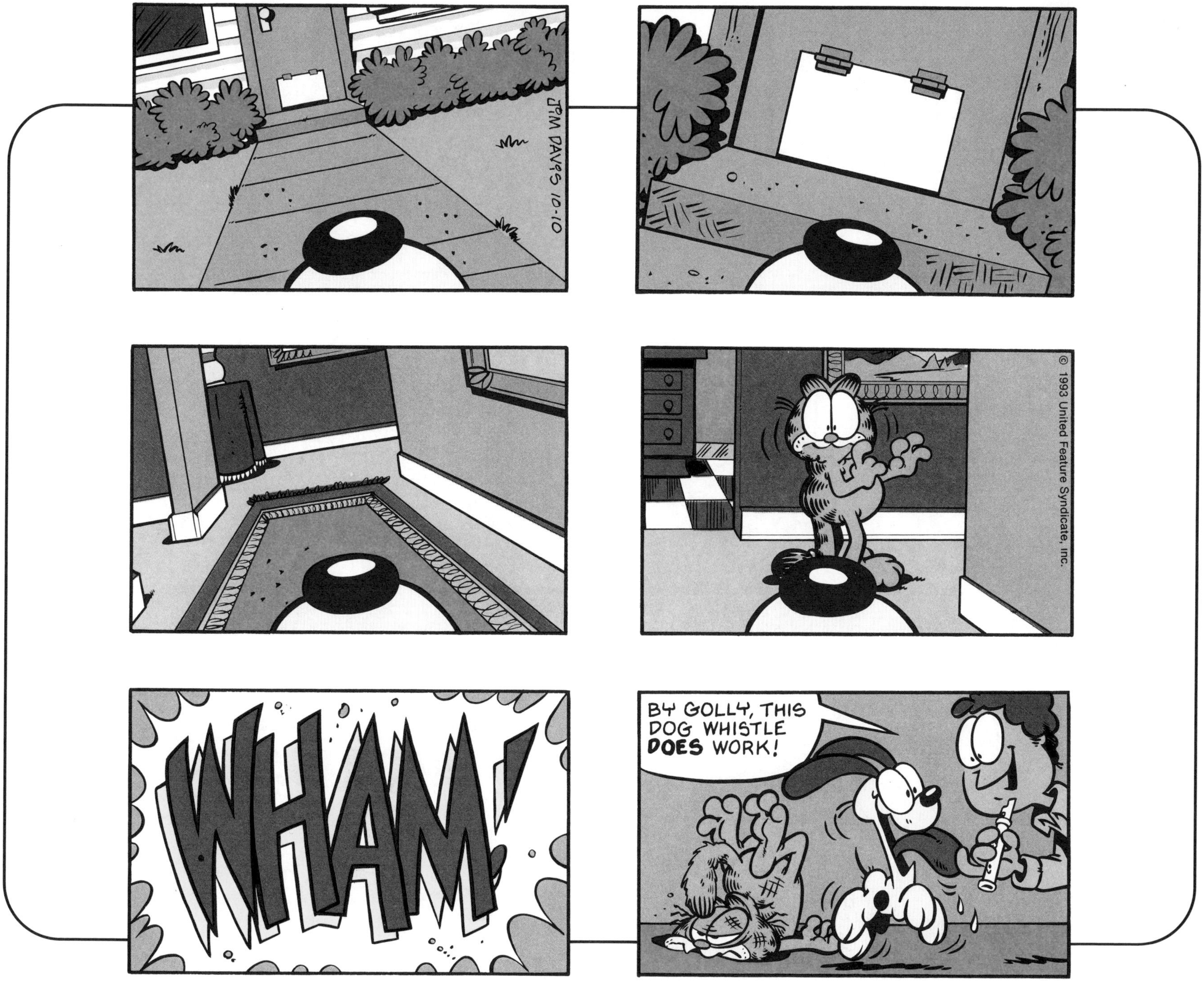
JIM DAVIS 10-10
© 1993 United Feature Syndicate, inc.
WHAM!
BY GOLLY, THIS DOG WHISTLE **DOES** WORK!

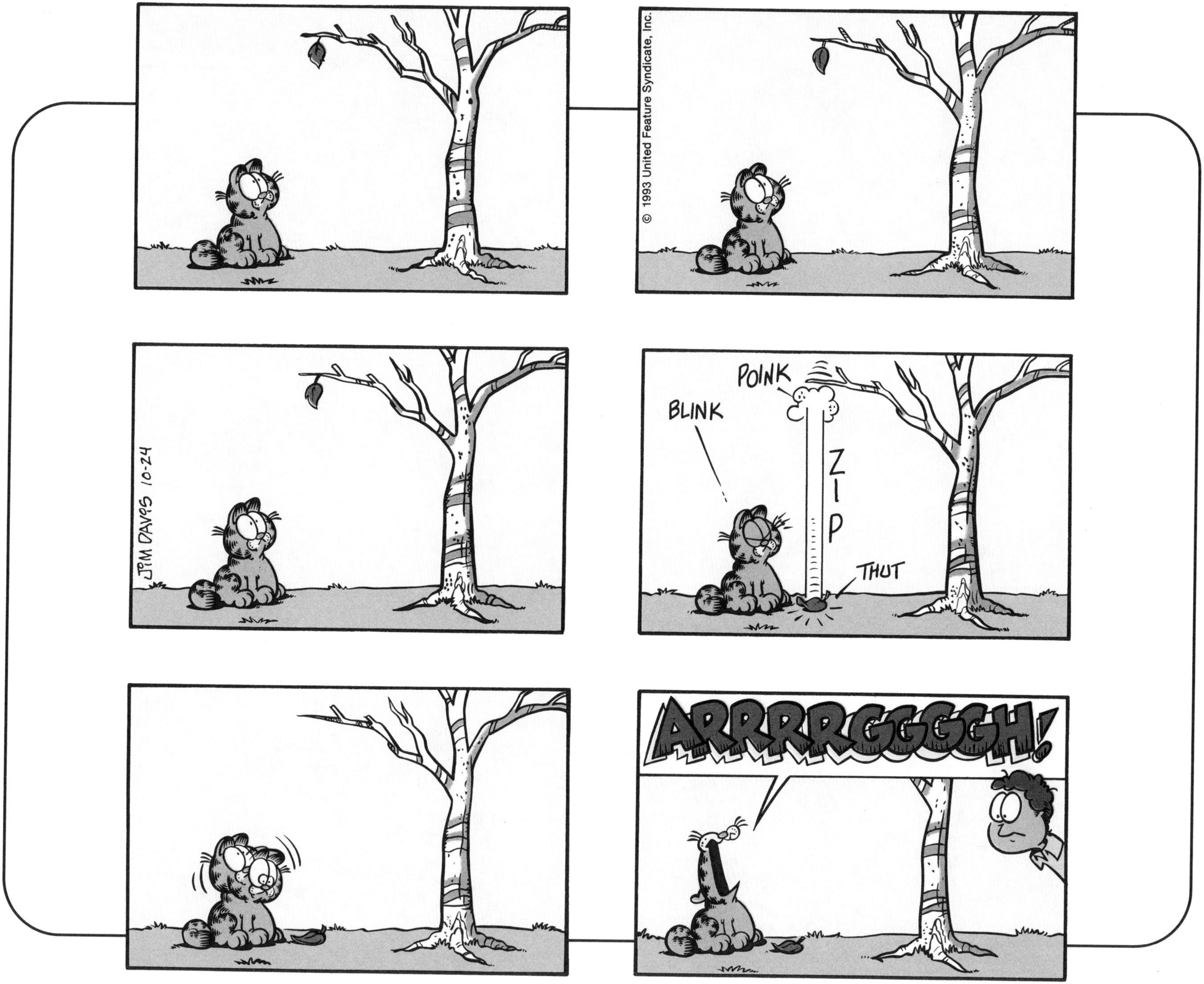
© 1993 United Feature Syndicate, Inc.
JIM DAVIS 10-24
BLINK
POINK
ZIP
THUT
ARRRRGGGGH!

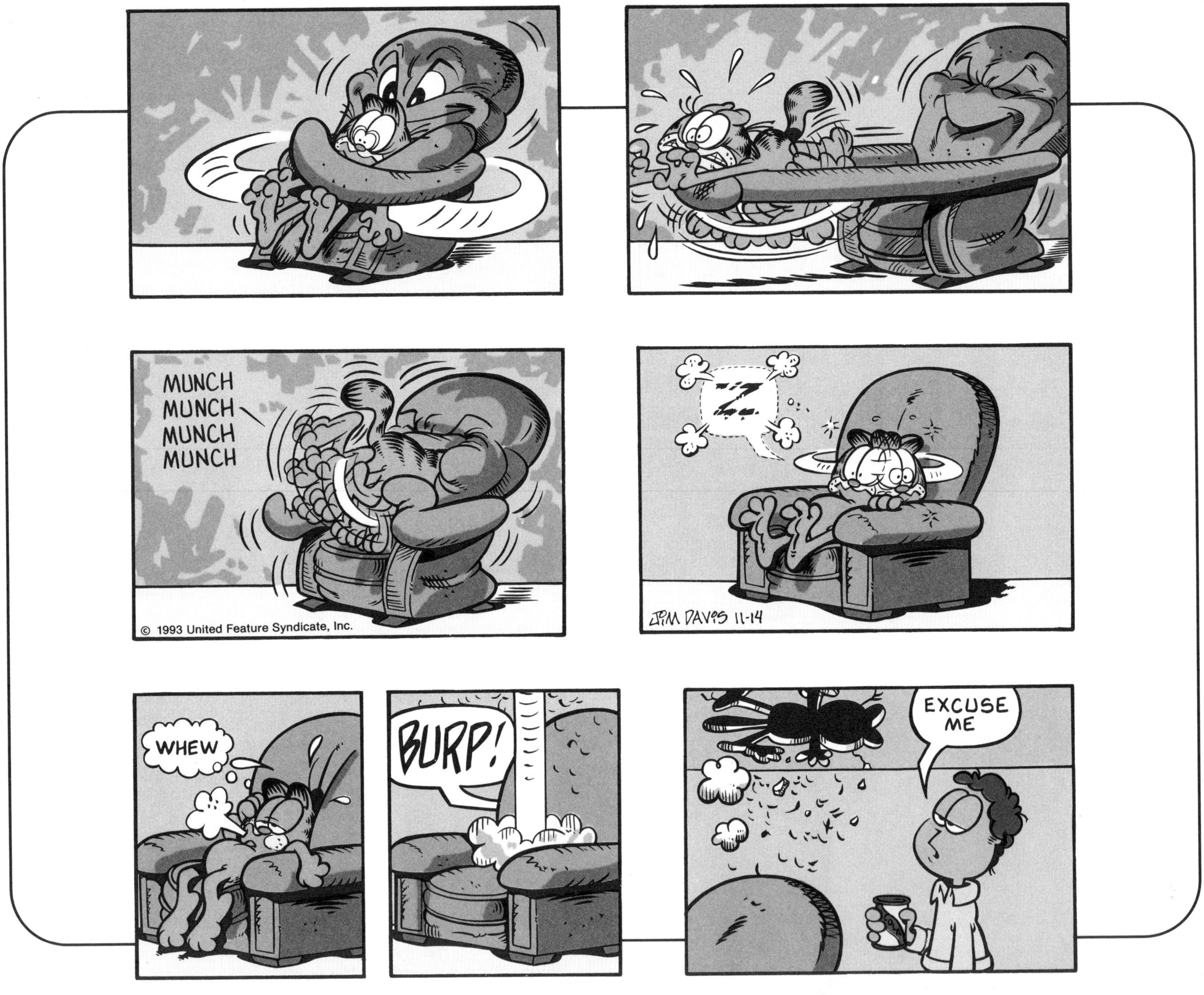
MUNCH
MUNCH
MUNCH
MUNCH
MUNCH
Z
JIM DAVIS 11-14
WHEW
BURP!
EXCUSE ME

© 1993 United Feature Syndicate, Inc.

I SUPPOSE WHEN YOU'RE THE FIRST SNOWFLAKE OF THE SEASON, YOU FEEL OBLIGATED TO MAKE A FLASHY ENTRANCE

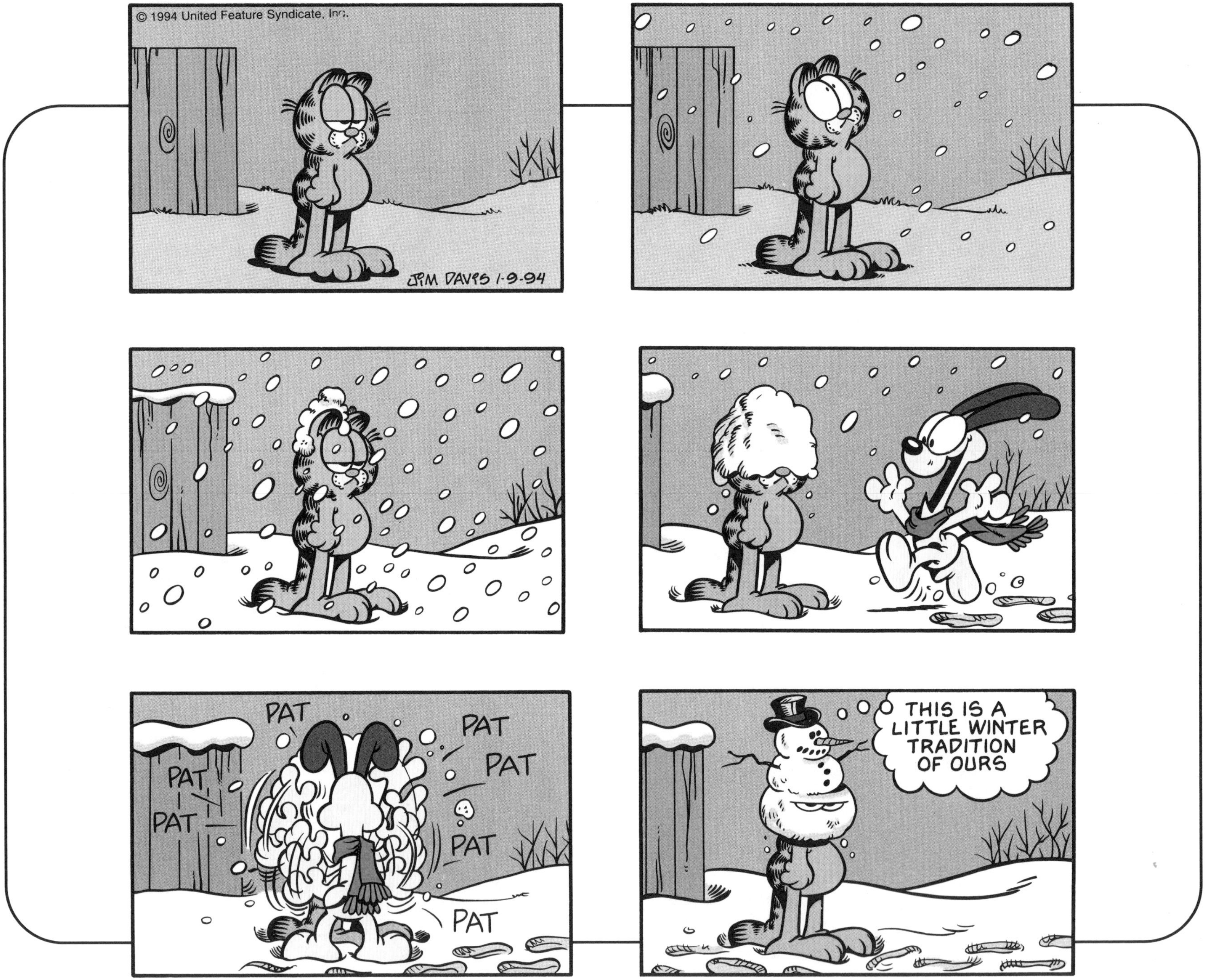
© 1994 United Feature Syndicate, Inc.
JIM DAVIS 1-9-94
PAT
PAT
PAT
PAT
PAT
PAT
PAT
THIS IS A LITTLE WINTER TRADITION OF OURS

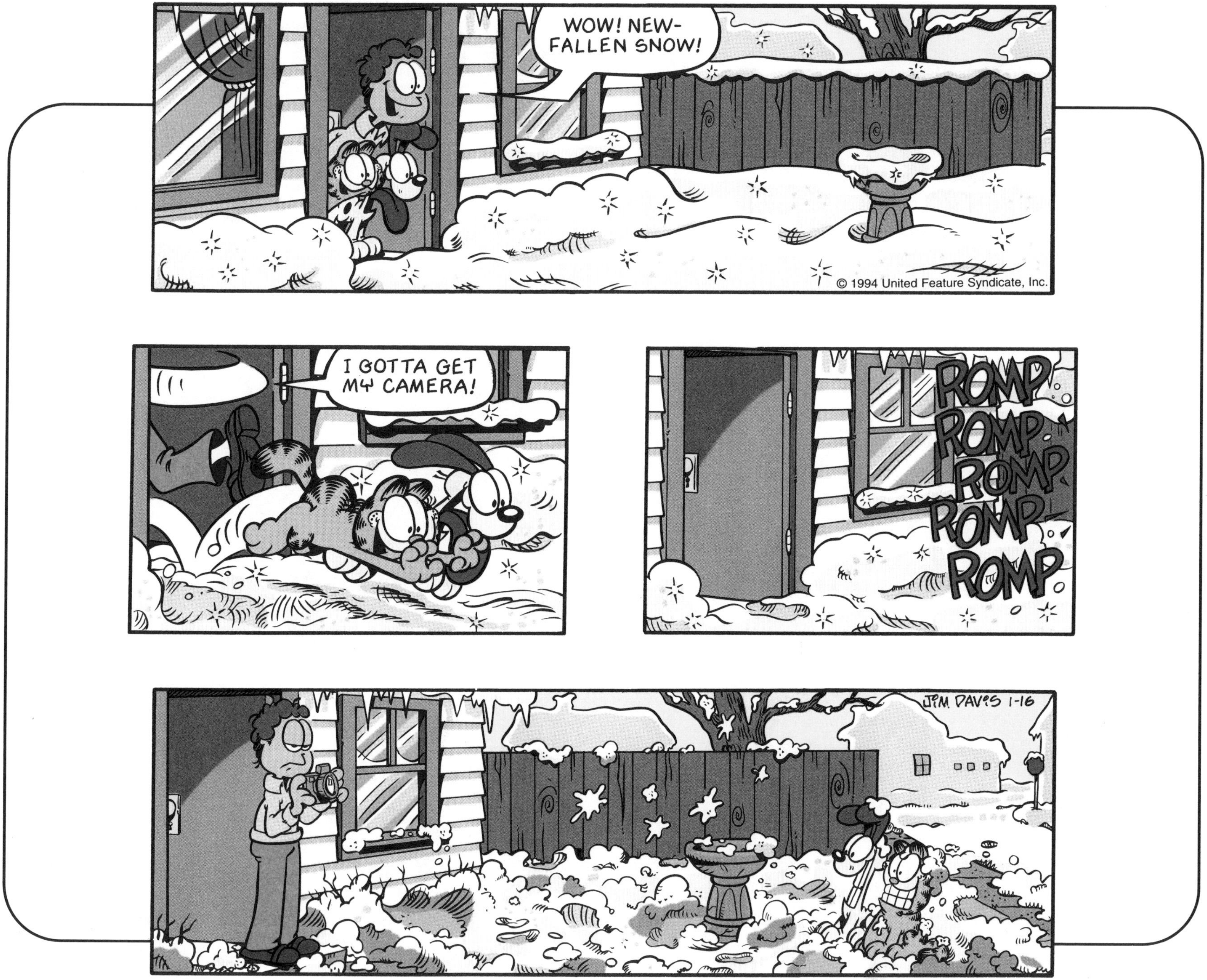
WOW! NEW-FALLEN SNOW!
© 1994 United Feature Syndicate, Inc.
I GOTTA GET MY CAMERA!
ROMP
ROMP
ROMP
ROMP
ROMP
JIM DAVIS 1-16

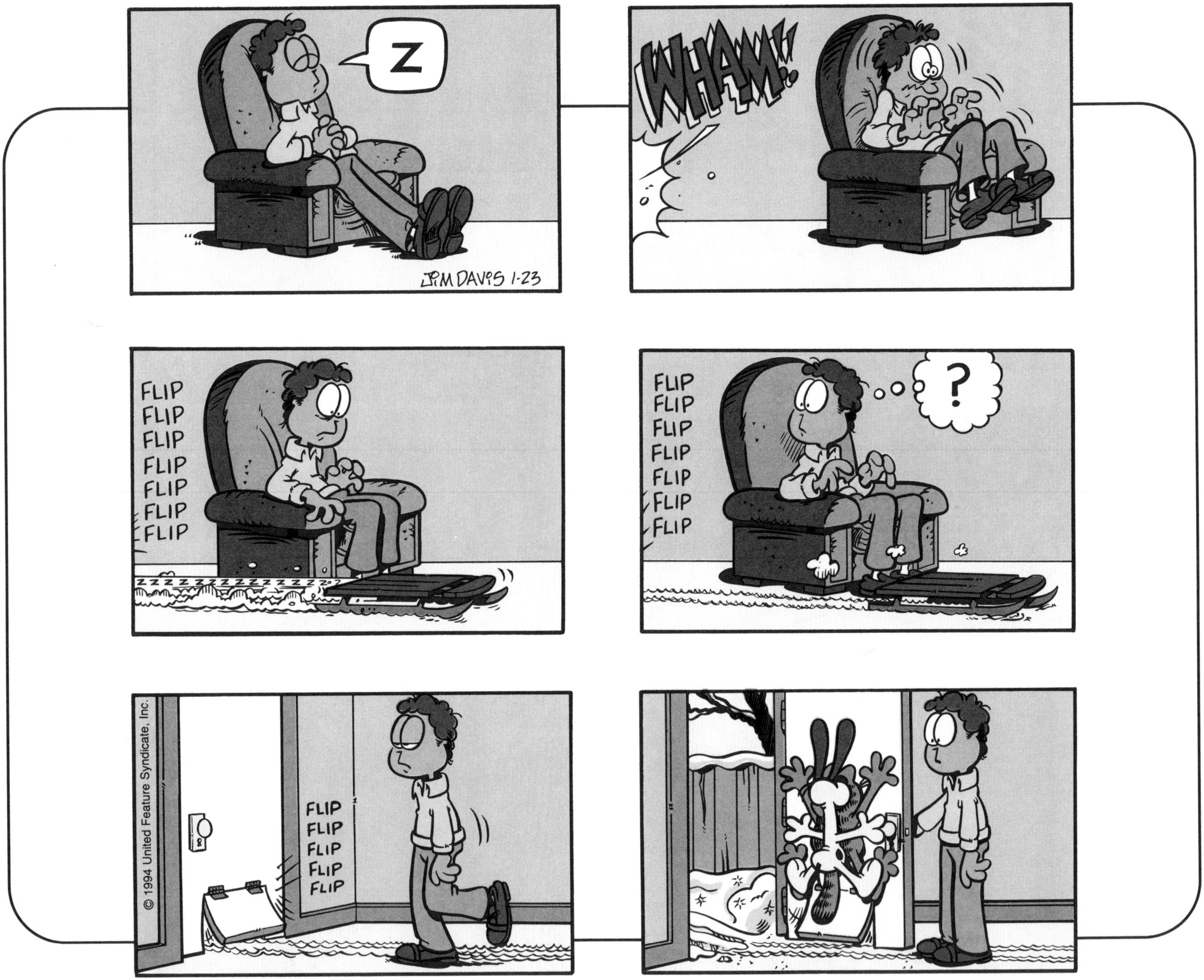
Z
JIM DAVIS 1-23
WHAM!!
FLIP FLIP FLIP FLIP FLIP FLIP FLIP
ZZZZZZZZZZZZZZZZ
FLIP FLIP FLIP FLIP FLIP FLIP FLIP
?
© 1994 United Feature Syndicate, Inc.
FLIP FLIP FLIP FLIP FLIP

© 1994 United Feature Syndicate, Inc.

JIM DAVIS 1-30

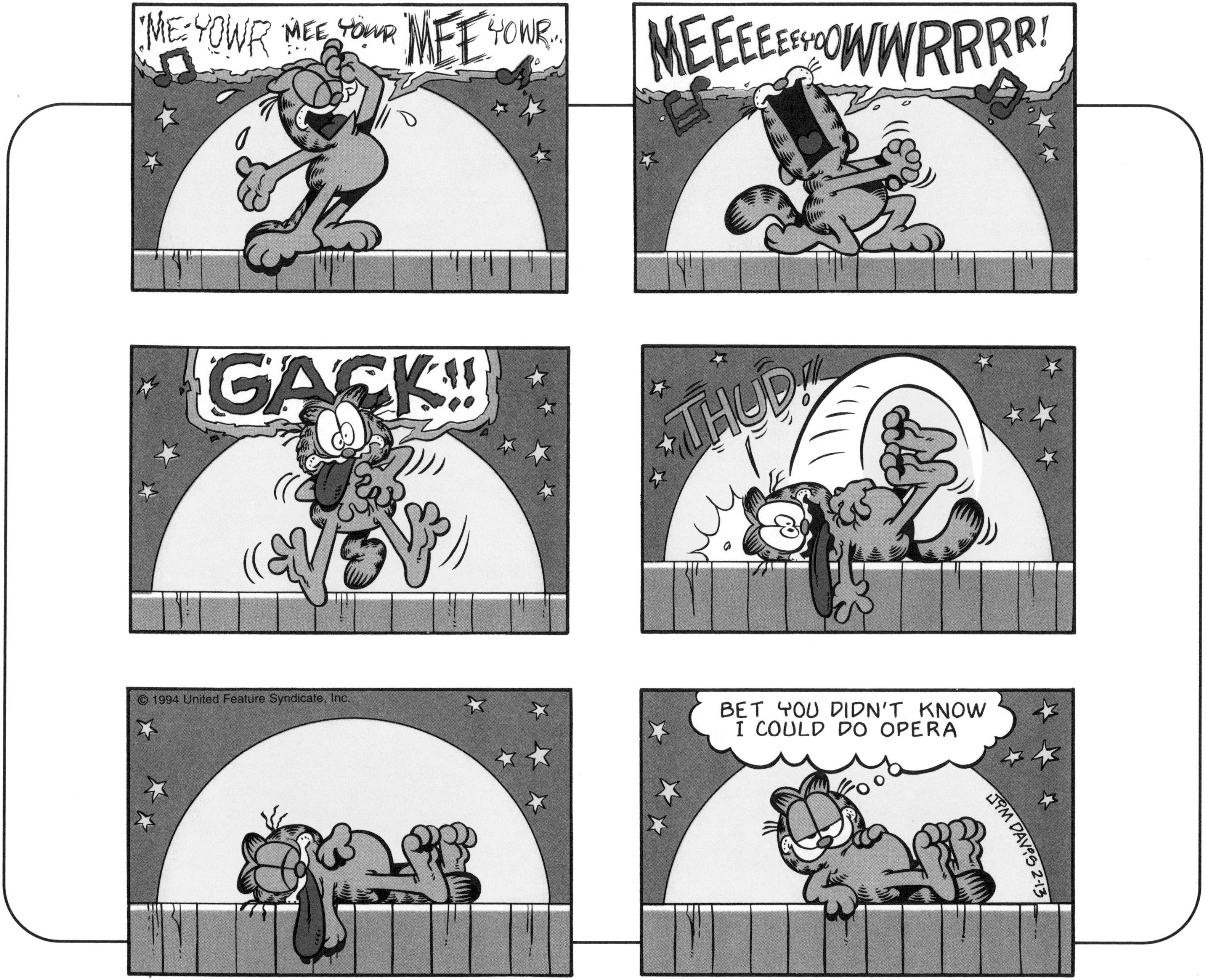
ME-YOWR MEE YOWR MEE YOWR...
MEEEEEEEYOOWWRRRRR!
GACK!!
THUD!
© 1994 United Feature Syndicate, Inc.
BET YOU DIDN'T KNOW I COULD DO OPERA
JIM DAVIS 2-13

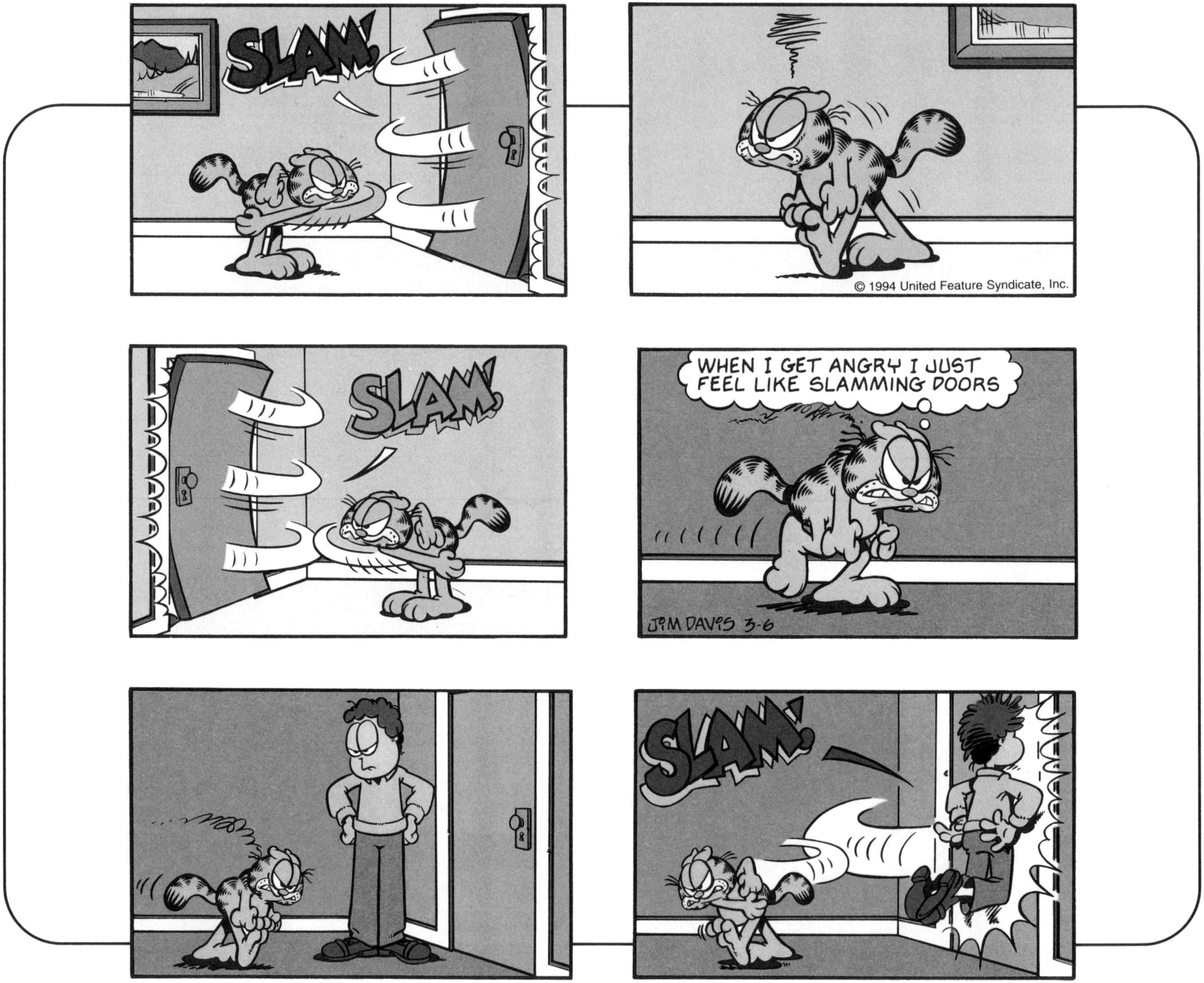
SLAM!
SLAM!
WHEN I GET ANGRY I JUST FEEL LIKE SLAMMING DOORS
JIM DAVIS 3-6
SLAM!
© 1994 United Feature Syndicate, Inc.

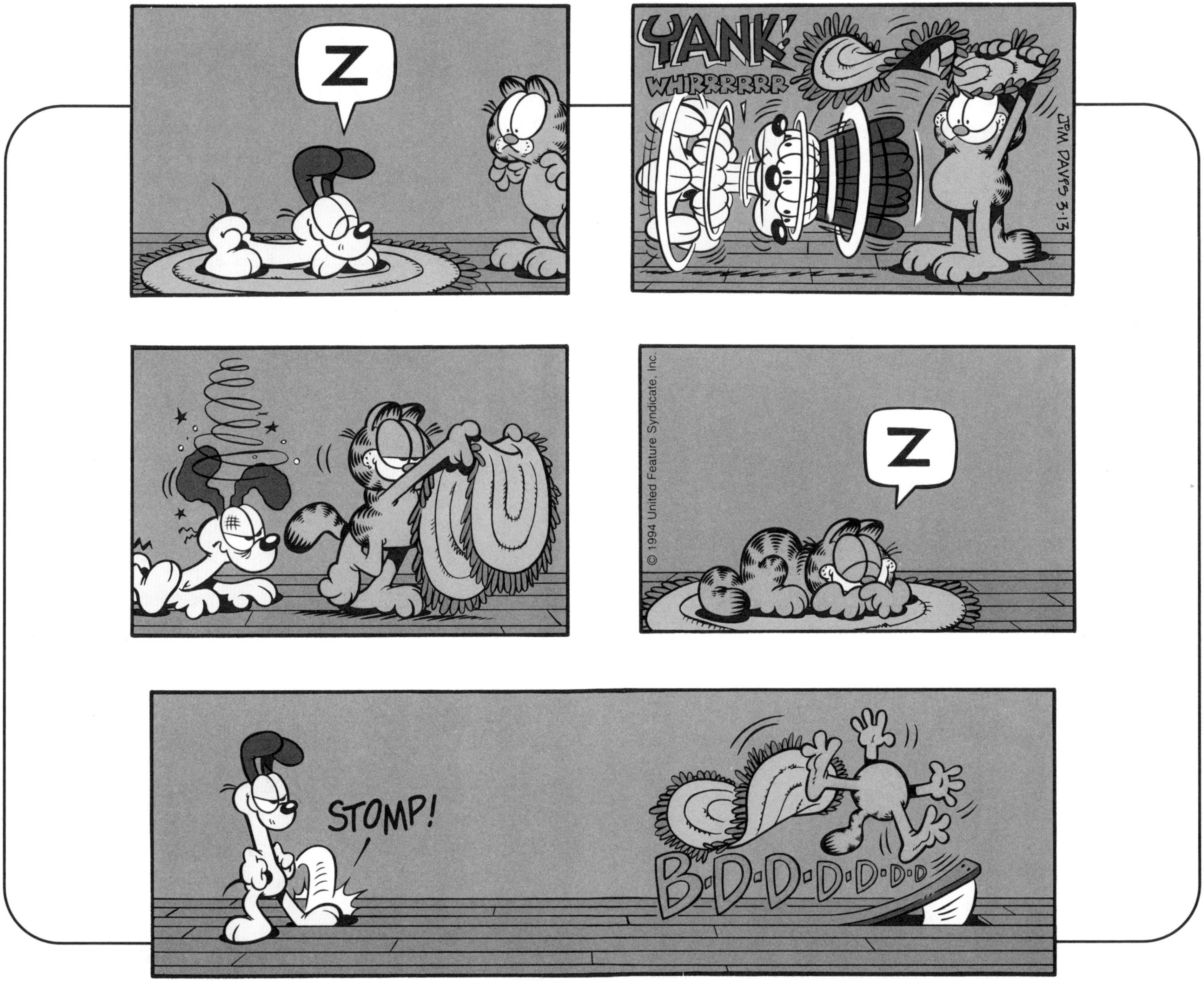
Z
YANK!
WHIRRRRRR
JIM DAVIS 3-13
© 1994 United Feature Syndicate, Inc.
Z
STOMP!
B-D-D-D-D-D-D

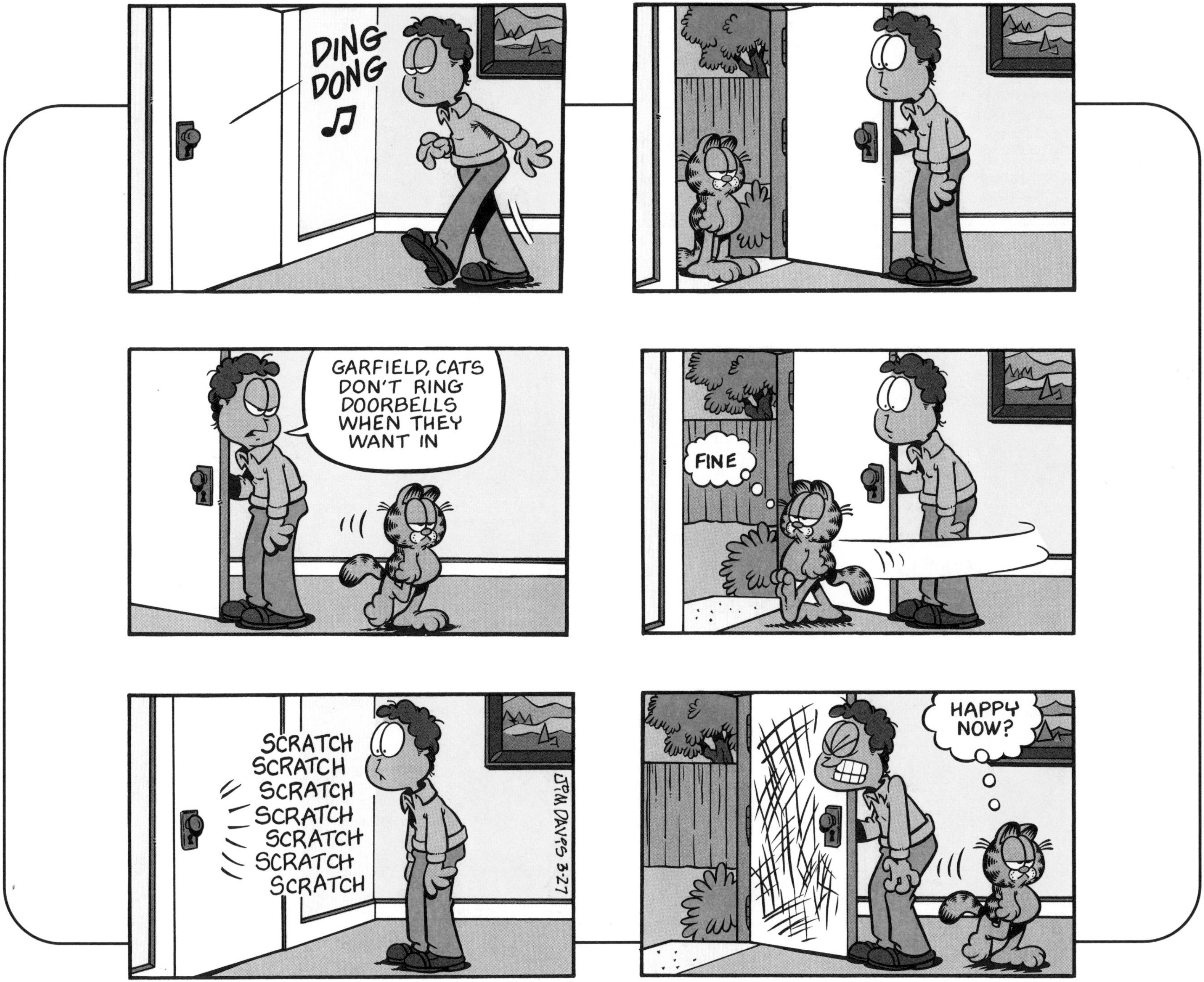
DING DONG ♫
GARFIELD, CATS DON'T RING DOORBELLS WHEN THEY WANT IN
FINE
SCRATCH SCRATCH SCRATCH SCRATCH SCRATCH SCRATCH SCRATCH
JPM DAVIS 3-27
HAPPY NOW?

JIM DAVIS 4-3

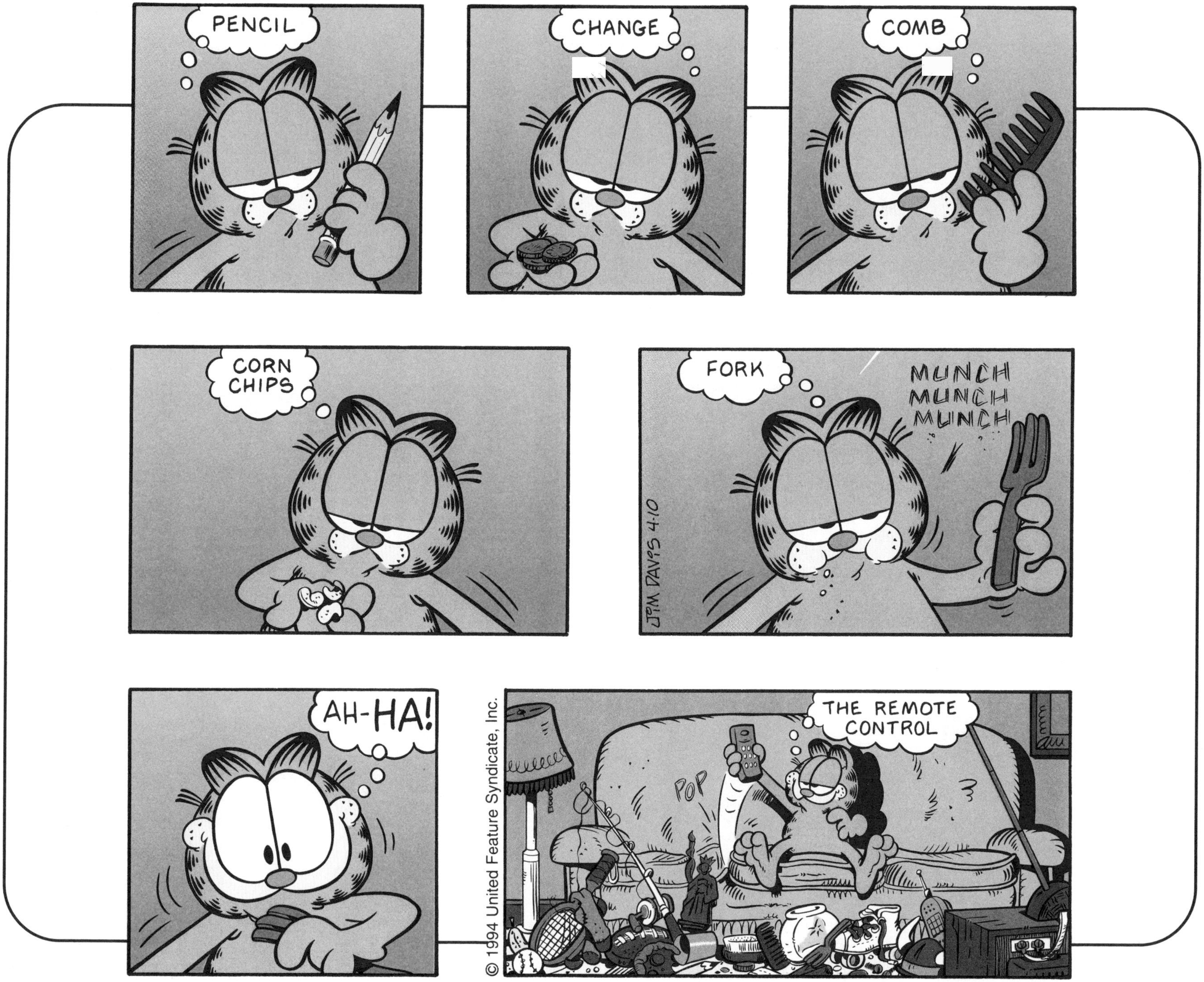
PENCIL
CHANGE
COMB
CORN CHIPS
FORK
MUNCH MUNCH MUNCH
JIM DAVIS 4-10
AH-HA!
THE REMOTE CONTROL
POP

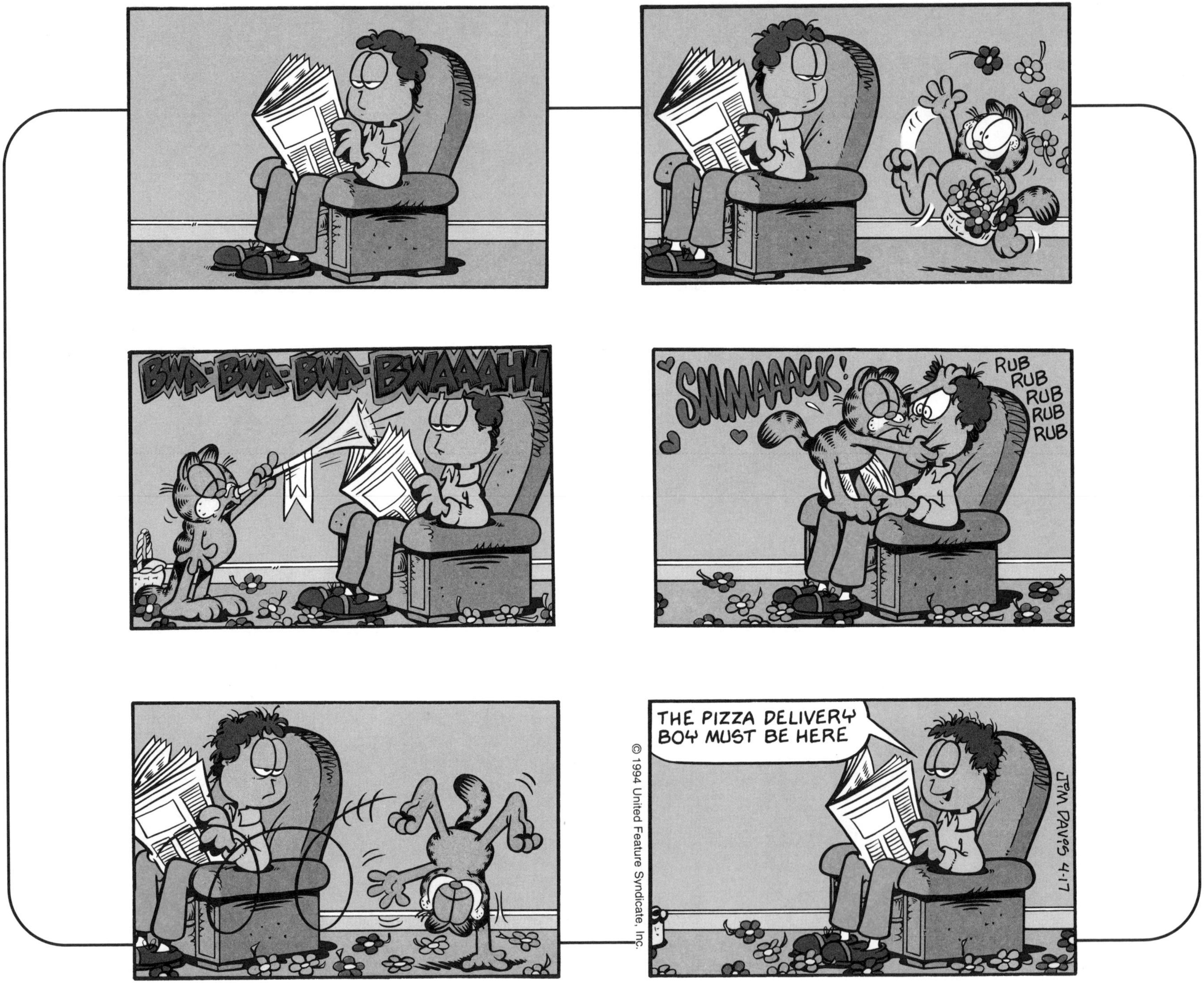
BWA-BWA-BWA-BWAAAHH
SMMAAACK!
RUB RUB RUB RUB RUB
THE PIZZA DELIVERY BOY MUST BE HERE
JPM DAVIS 4-17

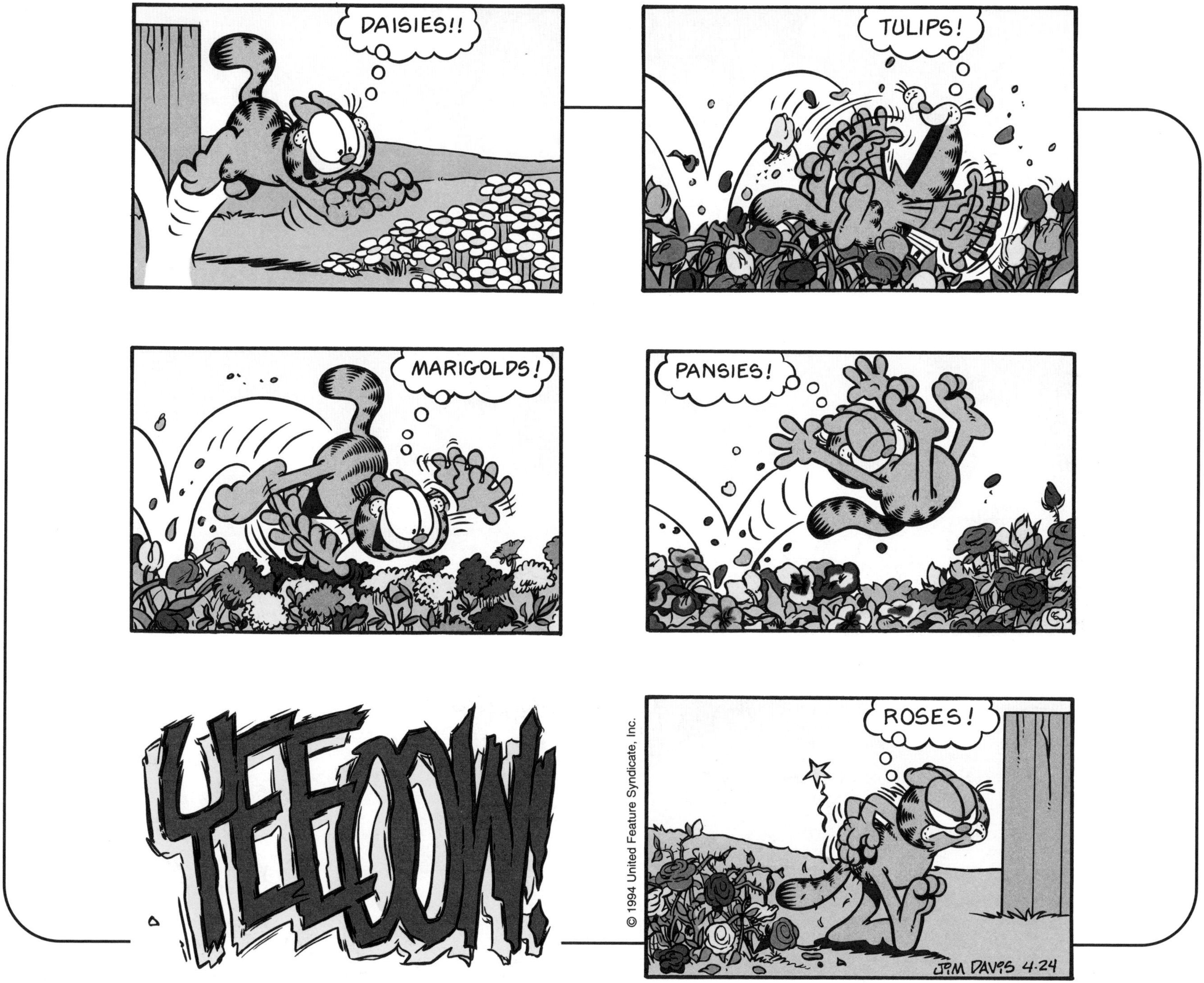
DAISIES!!
TULIPS!
MARIGOLDS!
PANSIES!
YEEOOW!
ROSES!
JIM DAVIS 4-24
© 1994 United Feature Syndicate, Inc.

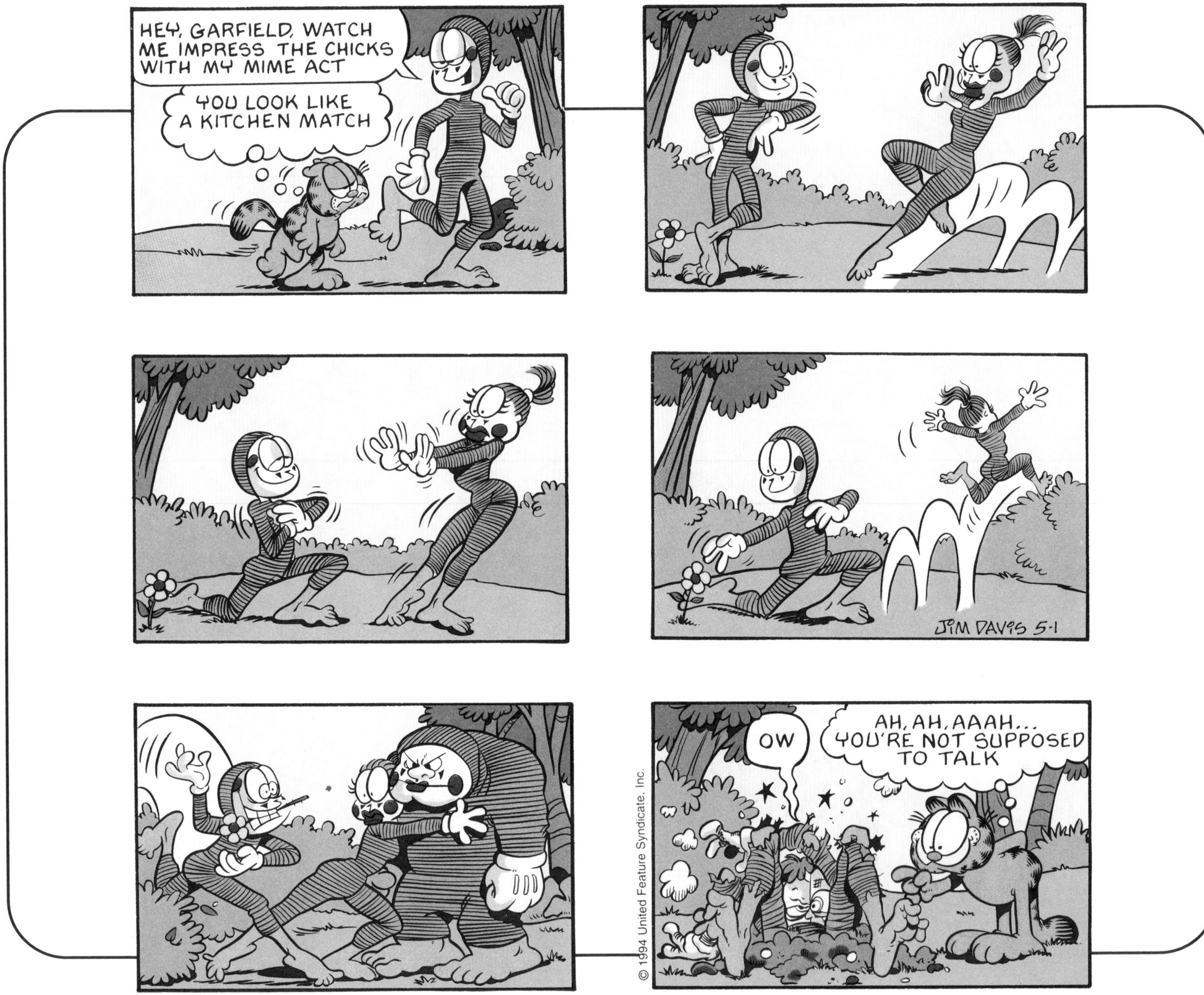
HEY, GARFIELD, WATCH ME IMPRESS THE CHICKS WITH MY MIME ACT
YOU LOOK LIKE A KITCHEN MATCH
JIM DAVIS 5-1
OW
AH, AH, AAAH... YOU'RE NOT SUPPOSED TO TALK

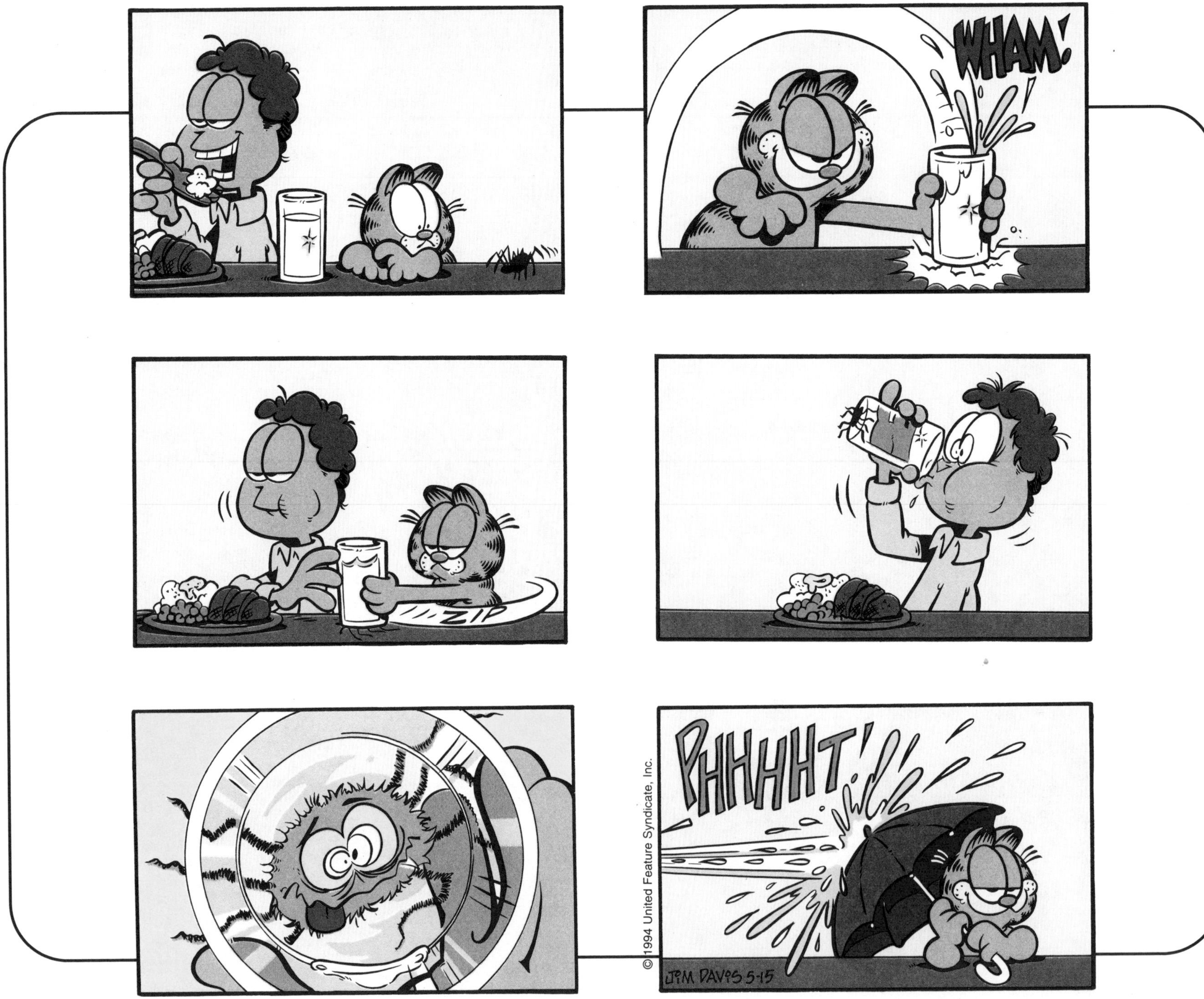
WHAM!
ZIP
PHHHT!
JIM DAVIS 5-15

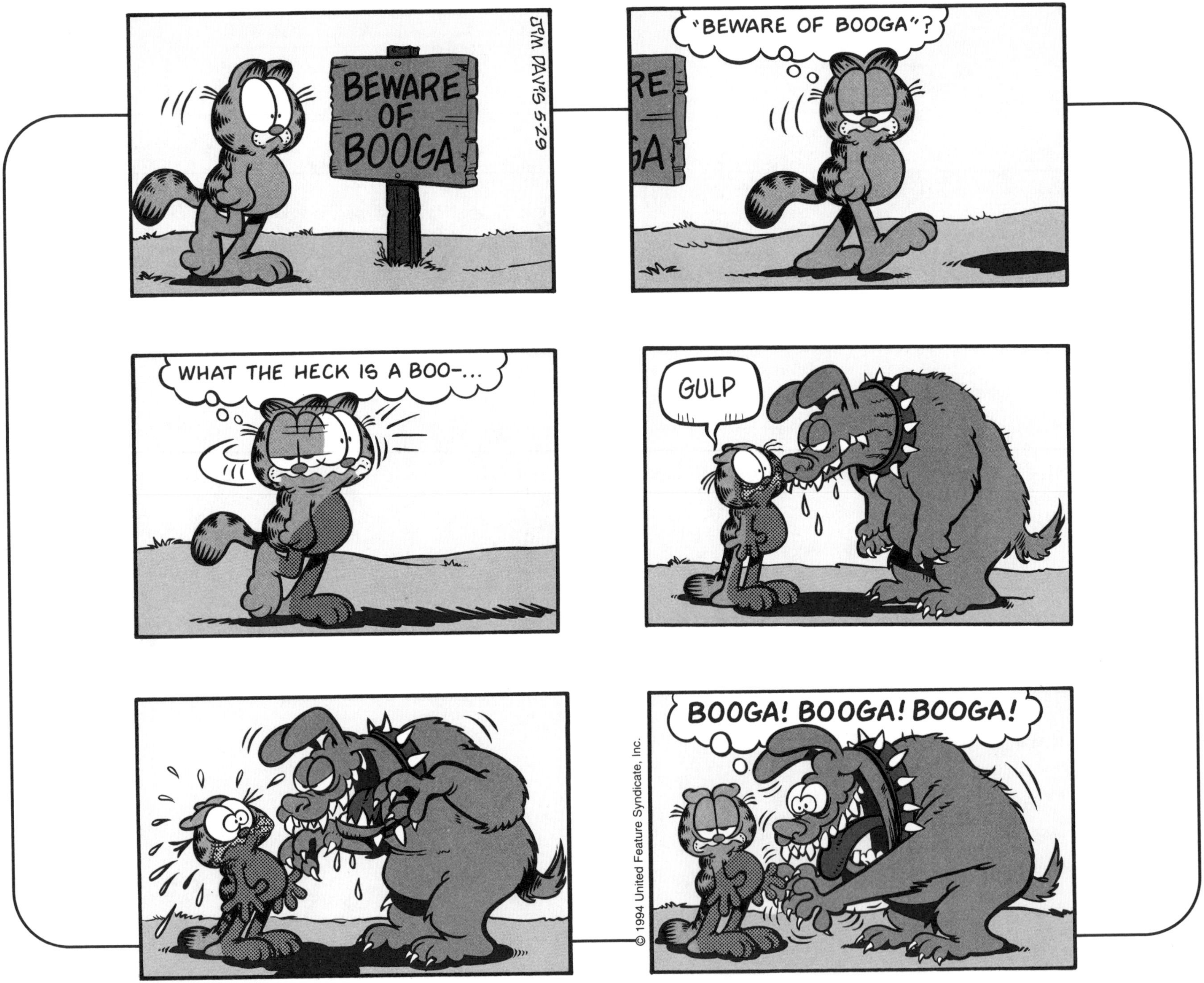
BEWARE OF BOOGA
JIM DAVIS 5-29
"BEWARE OF BOOGA"?
WHAT THE HECK IS A BOO-...
GULP
BOOGA! BOOGA! BOOGA!
© 1994 United Feature Syndicate, Inc.

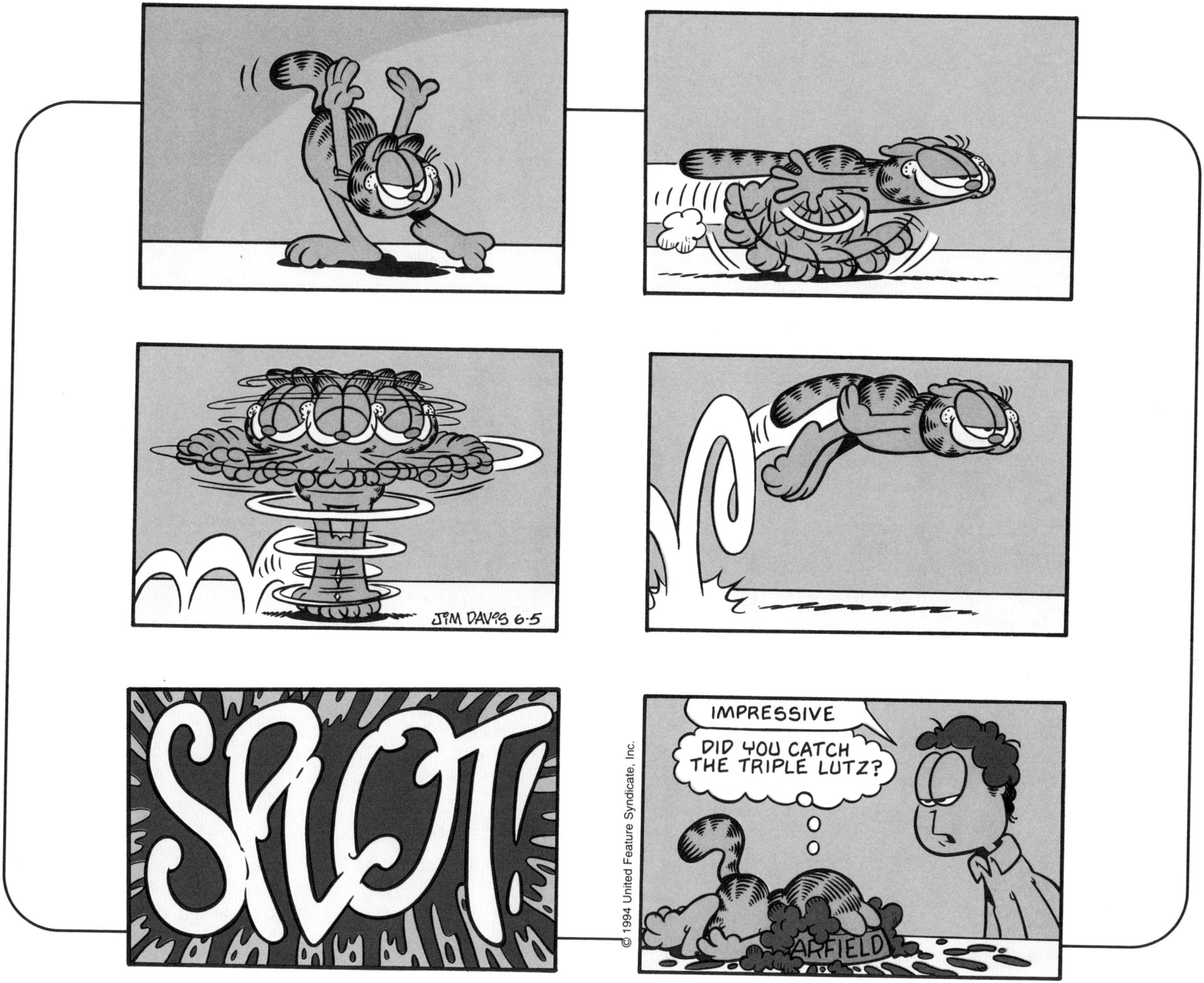
JIM DAVIS 6-5
SPLAT!
IMPRESSIVE
DID YOU CATCH THE TRIPLE LUTZ?
GARFIELD

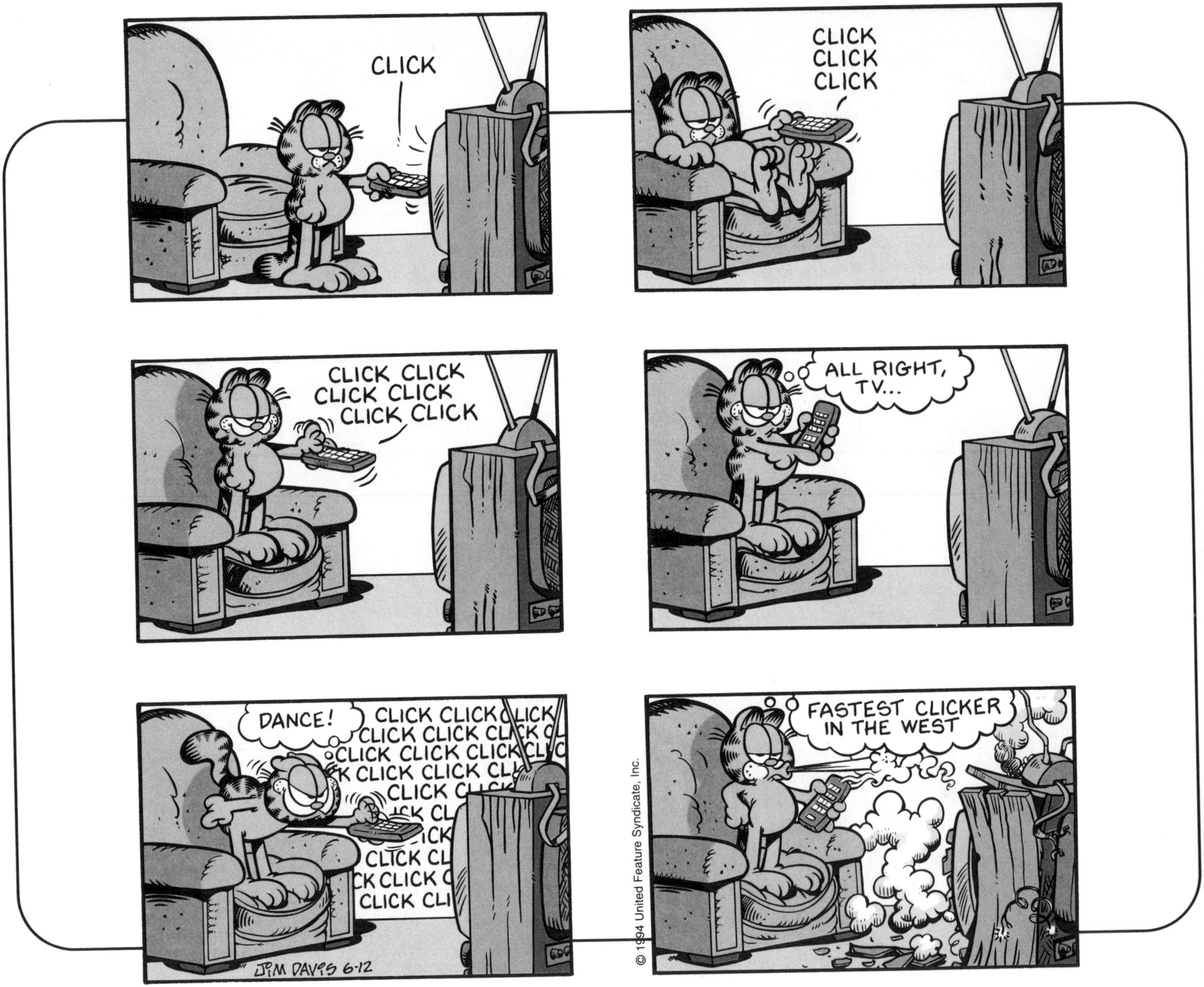
CLICK
CLICK CLICK CLICK
CLICK CLICK CLICK CLICK CLICK CLICK
ALL RIGHT, TV...
DANCE!
CLICK CLICK
CLICK CLICK
CLICK CLICK CLICK
CLICK CLICK
CLICK
CLICK
CLICK
CLICK
JIM DAVIS 6-12
FASTEST CLICKER IN THE WEST

© 1994 PAWS, INC./Distributed by Universal Press Syndicate

ALL RIGHT, GARFIELD. LET'S HAVE IT. SPIT IT OUT!

PTOO

SPLAT!

C'MON, THE REST OF IT!

PTOO

TAP TAP TAP

JIM DAVIS 6-26

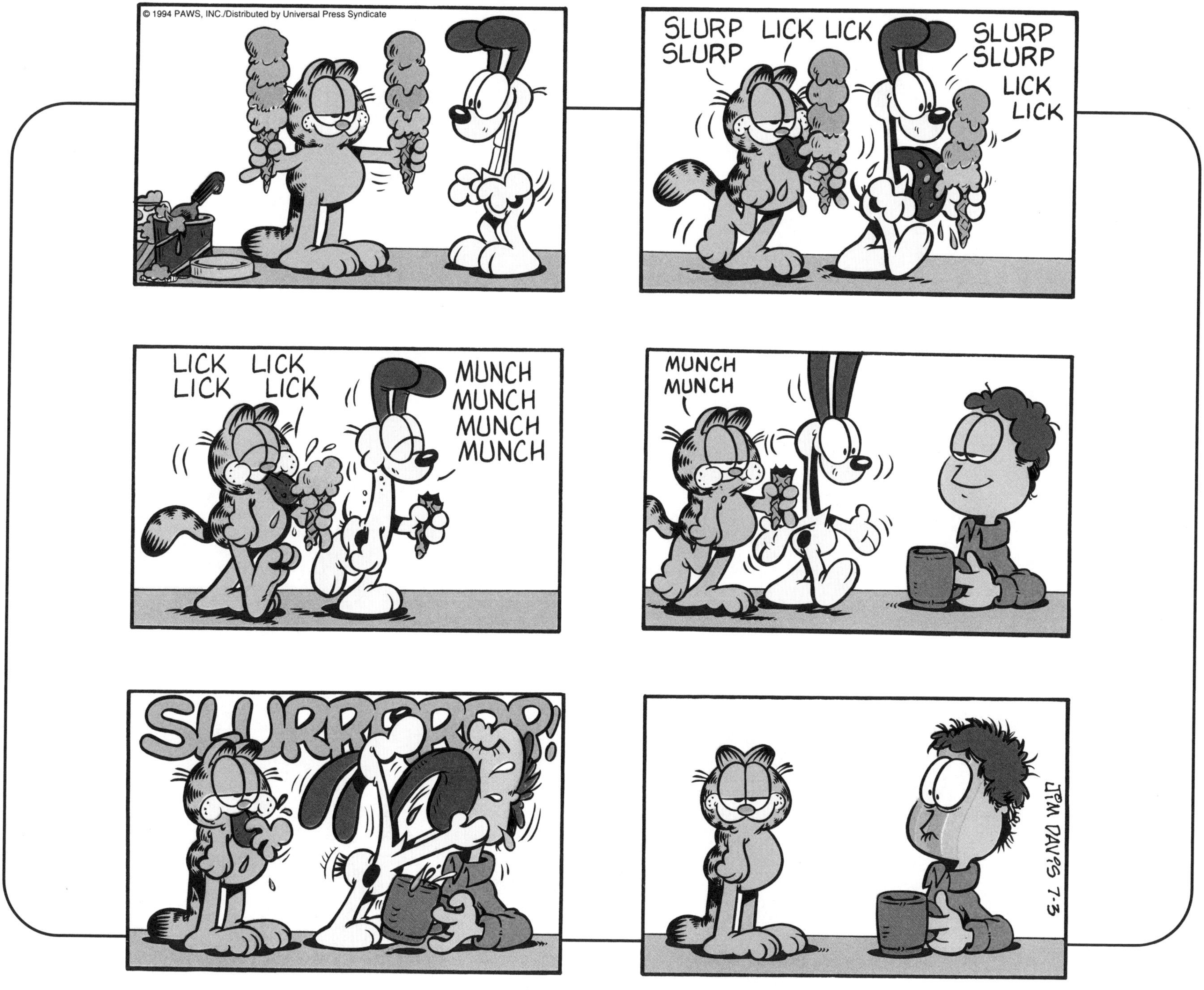

© 1994 PAWS, INC./Distributed by Universal Press Syndicate
SLURP SLURP
LICK LICK
SLURP SLURP
LICK LICK
LICK LICK
LICK LICK
MUNCH MUNCH MUNCH MUNCH
MUNCH MUNCH
SLURRRRP!
JIM DAVIS 7-3

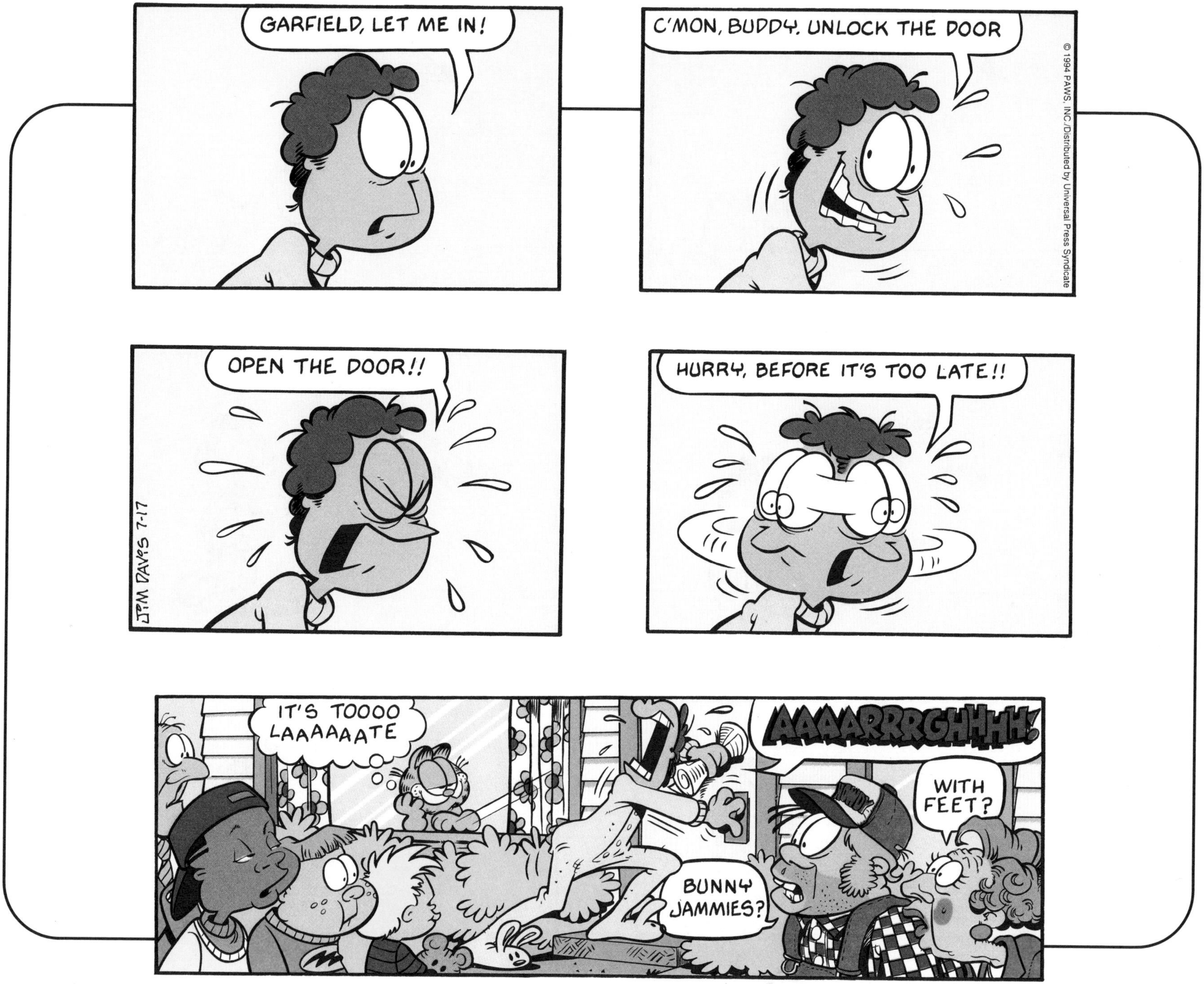
GARFIELD, LET ME IN!
C'MON, BUDDY. UNLOCK THE DOOR
OPEN THE DOOR!!
HURRY, BEFORE IT'S TOO LATE!!
JIM DAVIS 7-17
IT'S TOOOO LAAAAAATE
AAAARRRGHHHH!
WITH FEET?
BUNNY JAMMIES?

KLACK!

© 1994 PAWS, INC./Distributed by Universal Press Syndicate

JIM DAVIS 7-24

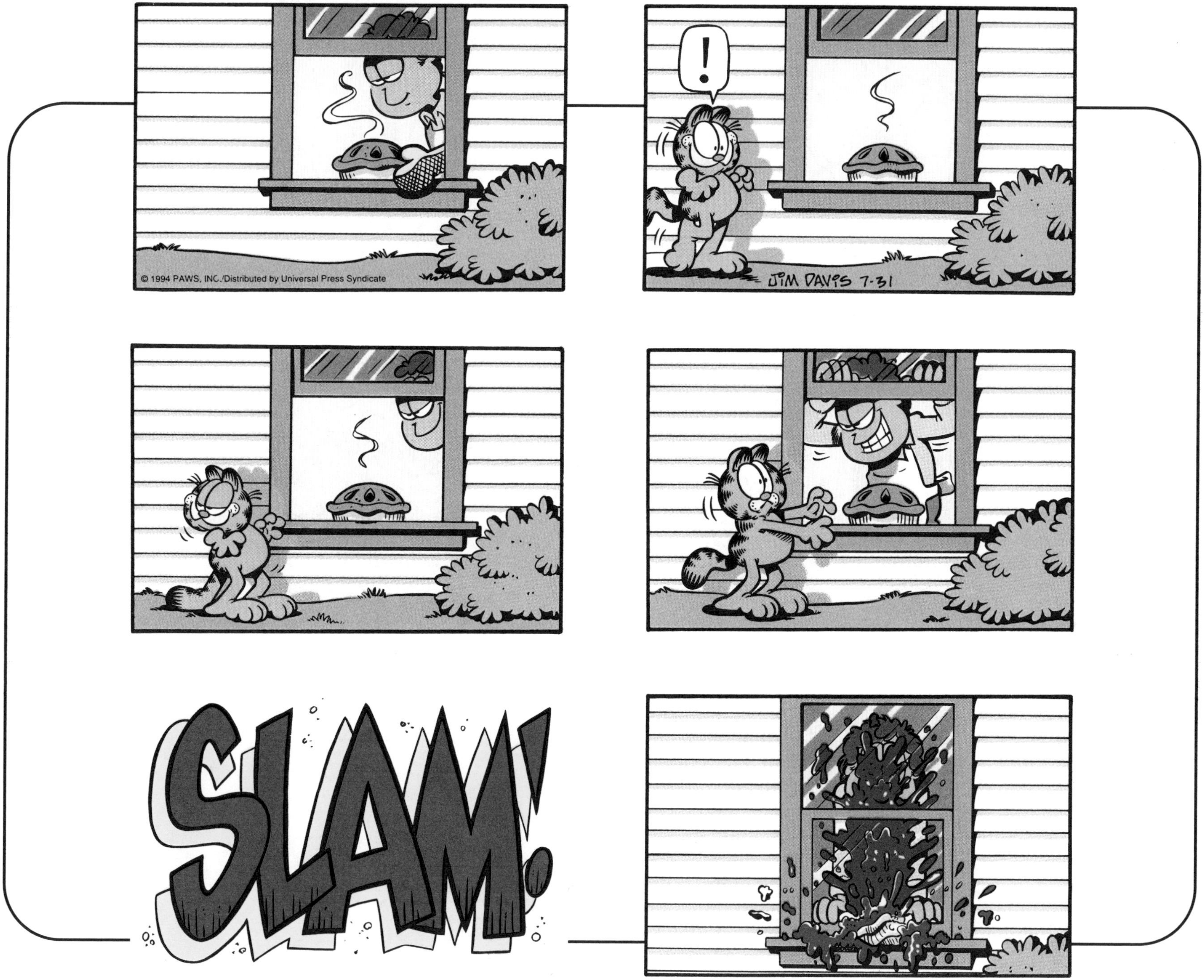

© 1994 PAWS, INC./Distributed by Universal Press Syndicate
!
JIM DAVIS 7-31
SLAM!

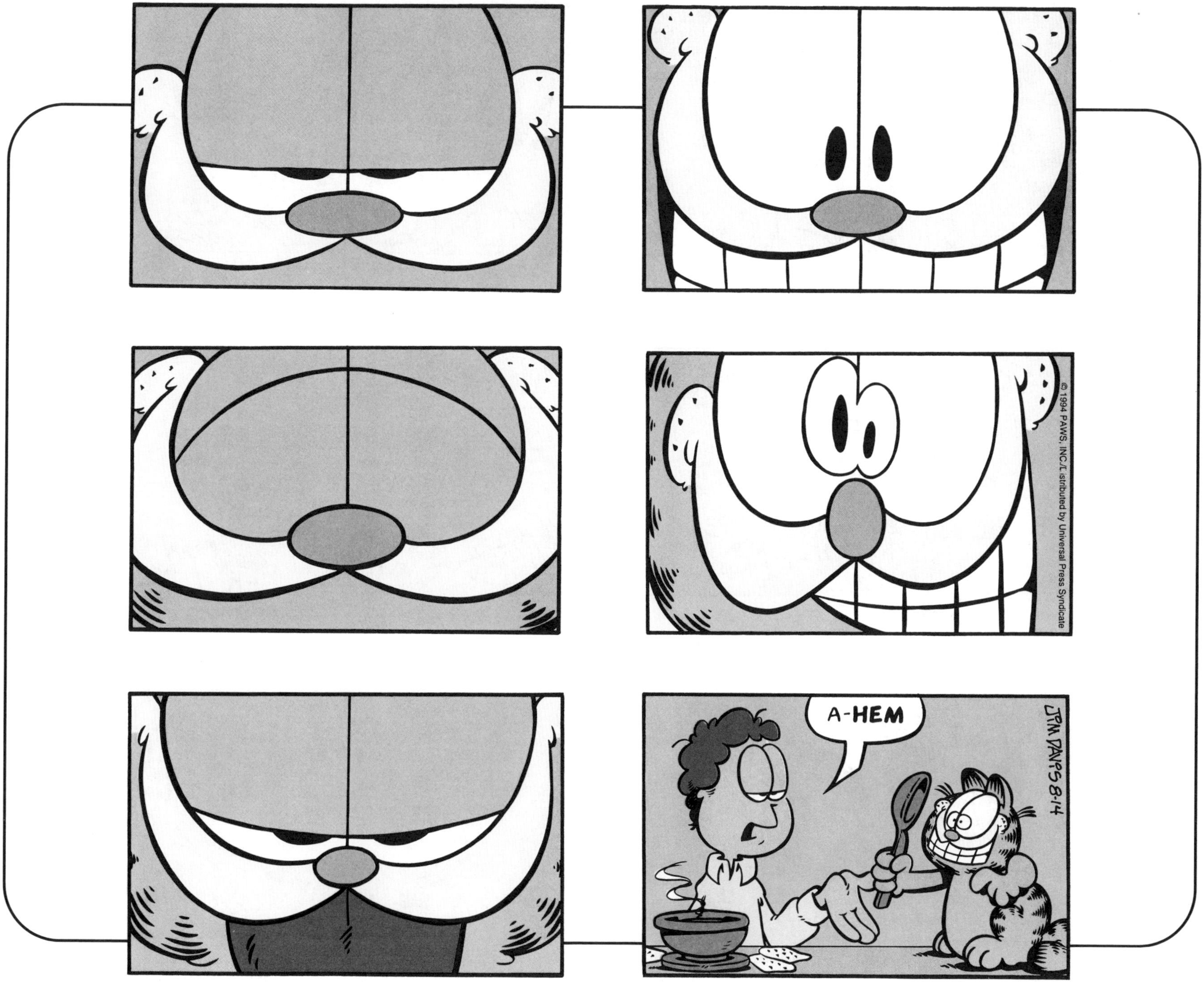
A-HEM
JIM DAVIS 8-14
© 1994 PAWS, INC./Distributed by Universal Press Syndicate

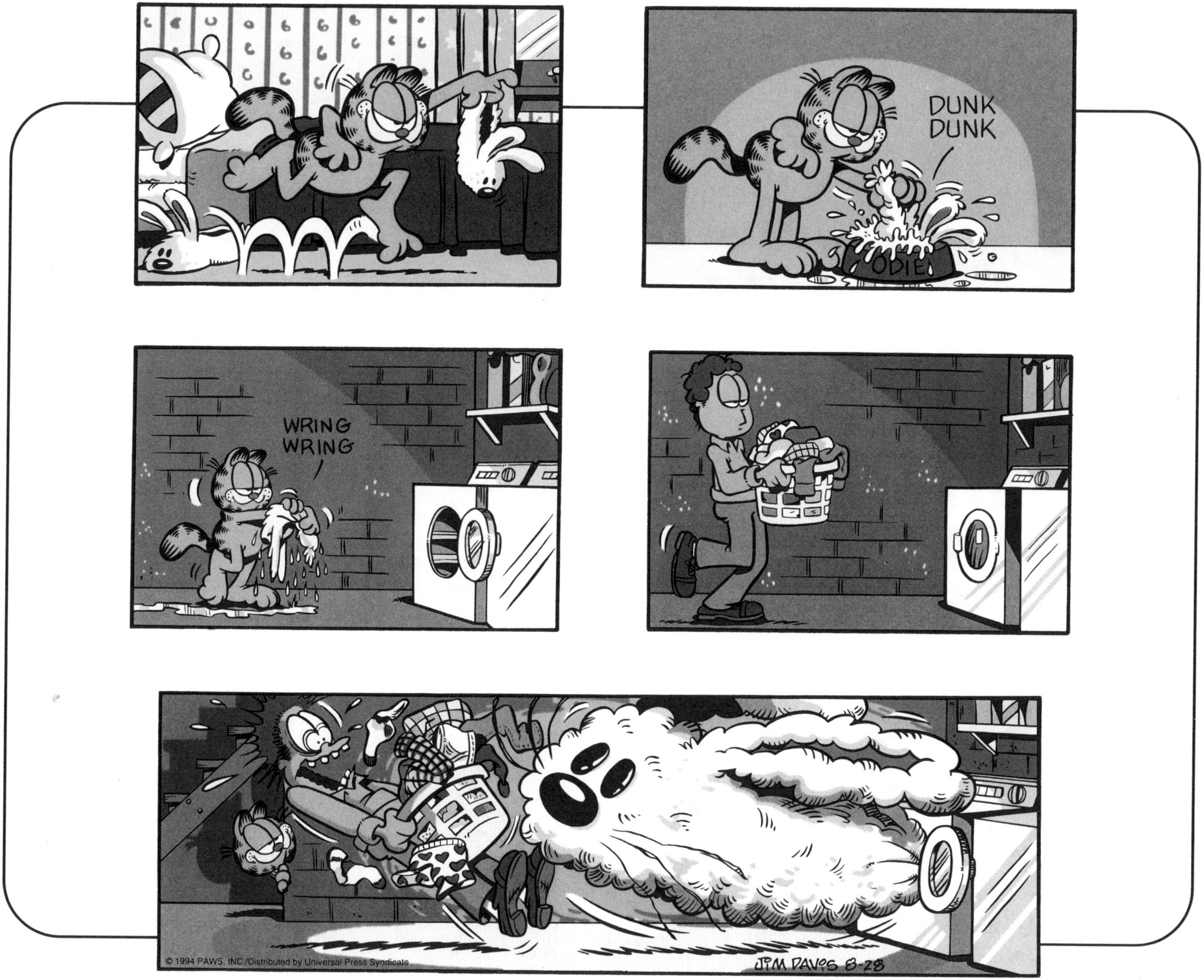
DUNK
DUNK
WRING
WRING
ODIE
© 1994 PAWS, INC./Distributed by Universal Press Syndicate
JIM DAVIS 8-28

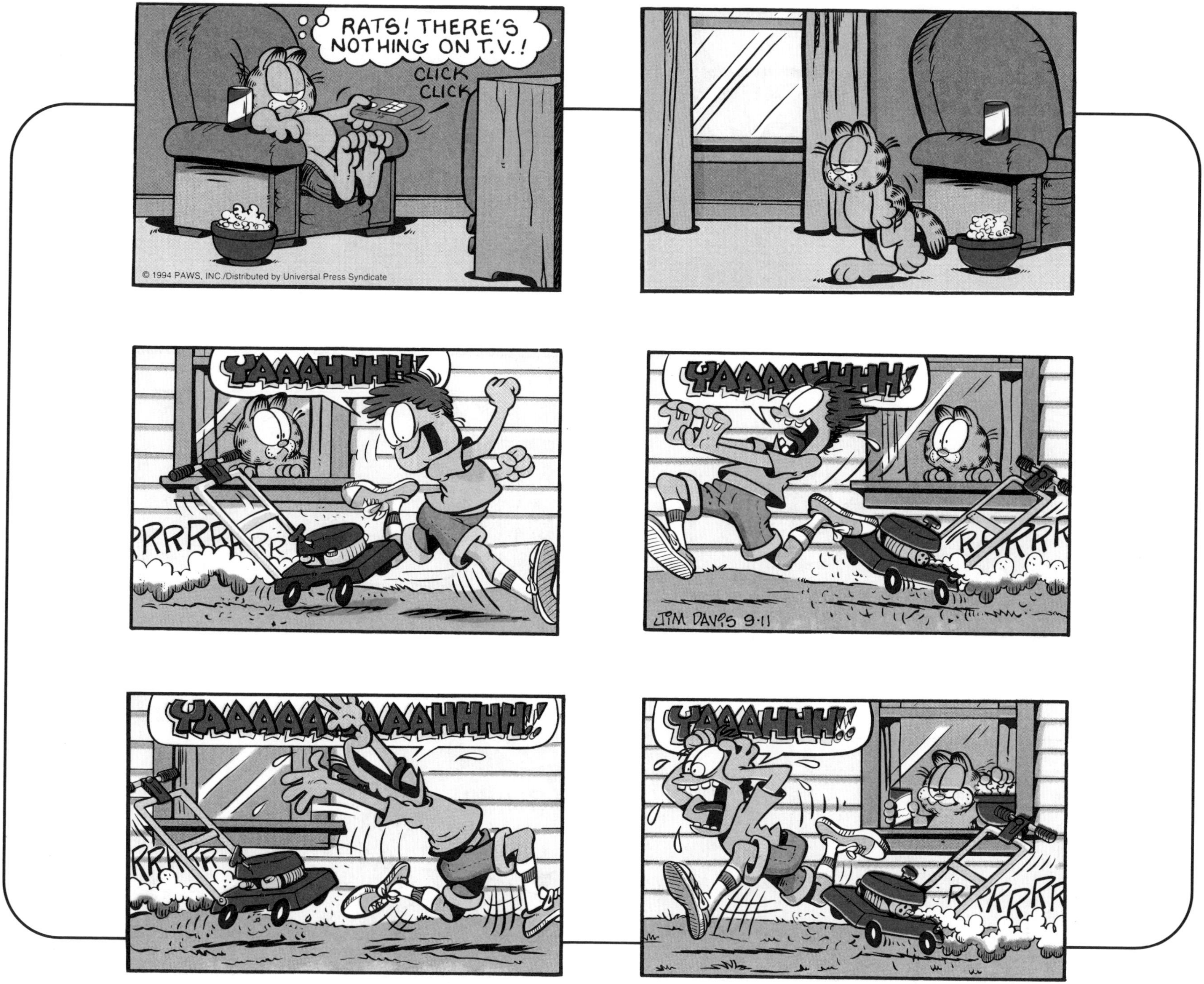
RATS! THERE'S NOTHING ON T.V.!
CLICK CLICK
© 1994 PAWS, INC./Distributed by Universal Press Syndicate
YAAAHHHH!
RRRRR
YAAAOUHH!
RRRRR
JIM DAVIS 9-11
YAAAAA AAAHHHH!!
RRRR
YAAAHHH!!
RRRRR

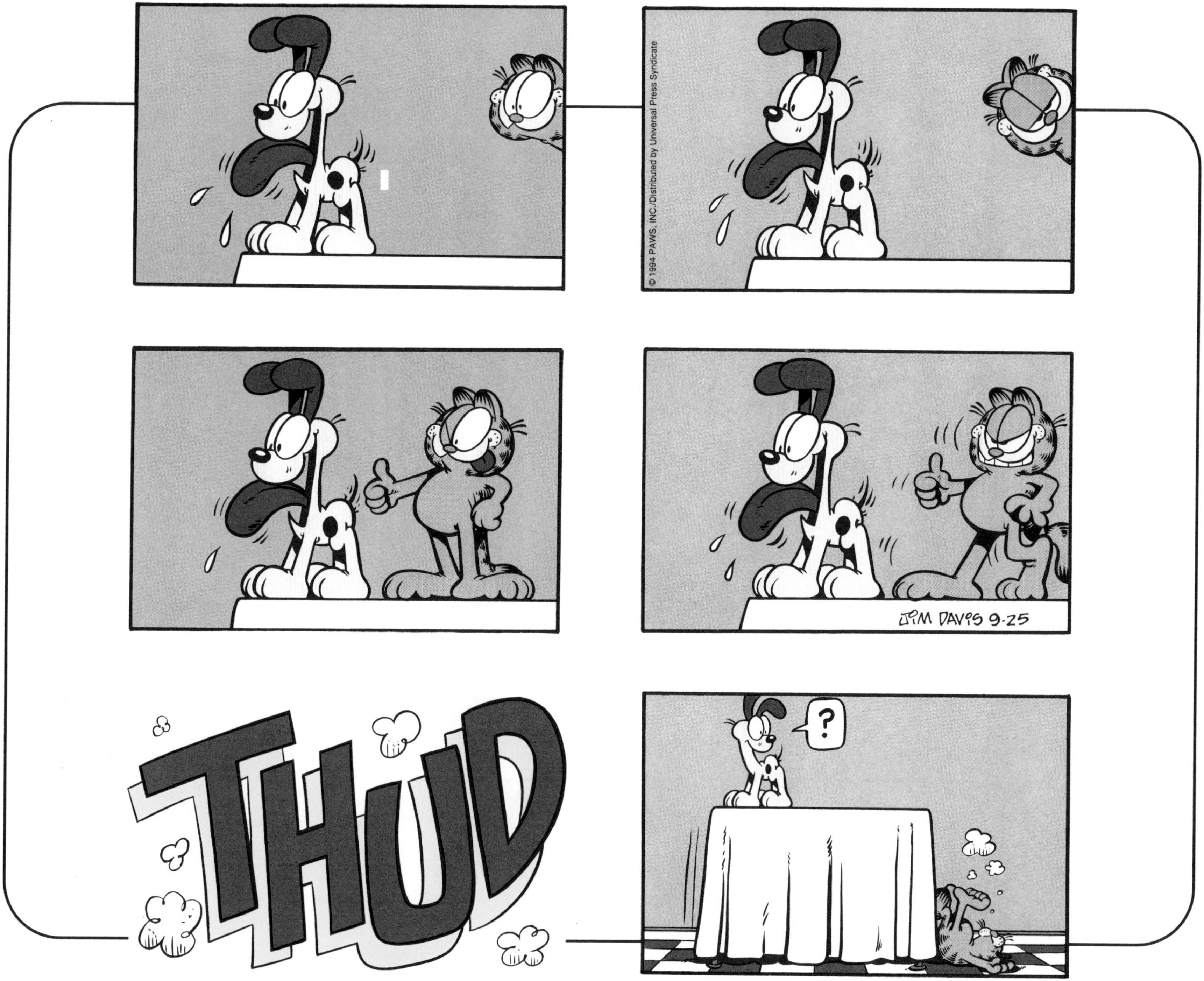
© 1994 PAWS, INC./Distributed by Universal Press Syndicate
JIM DAVIS 9-25
THUD
?

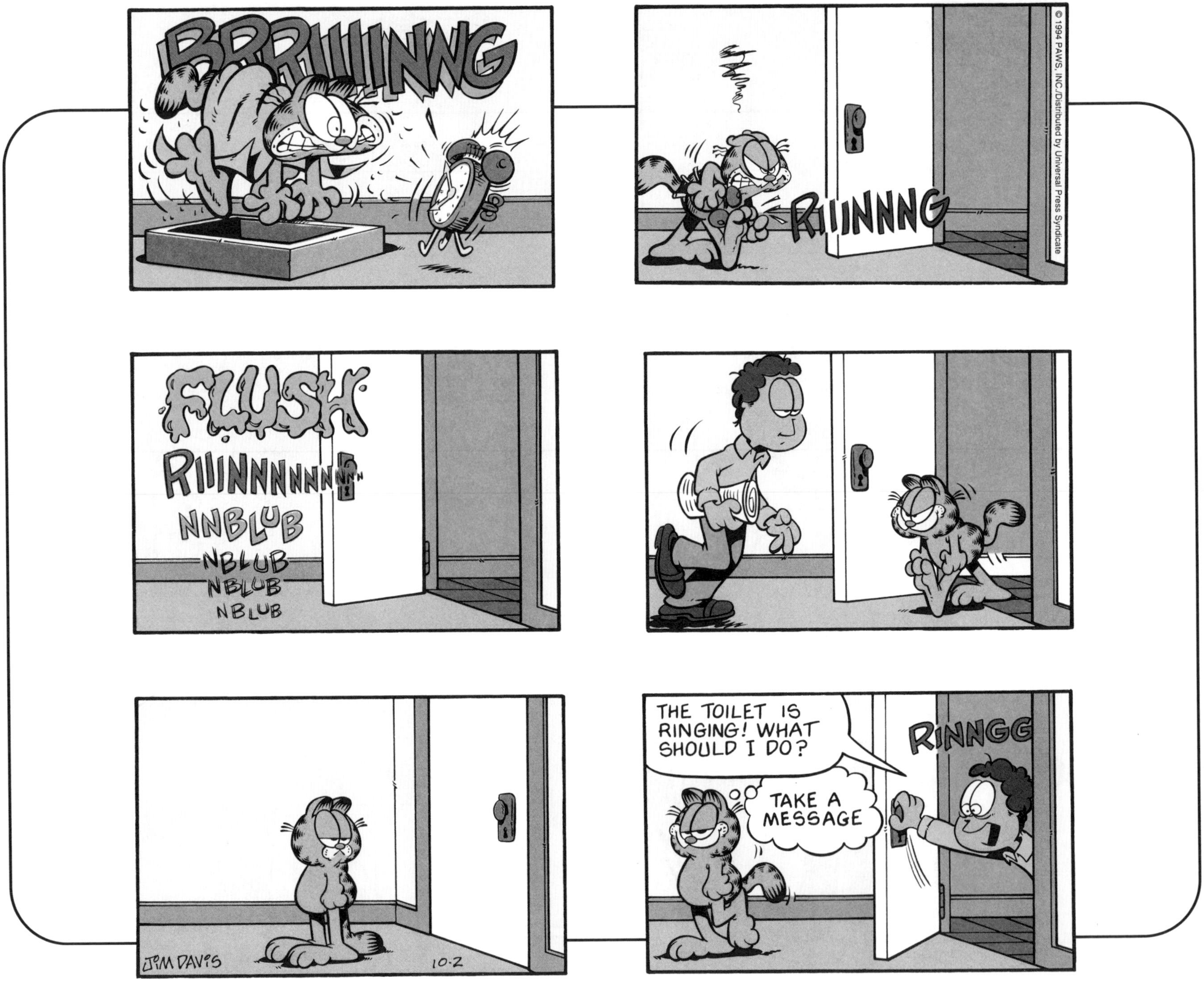
BRRIIIINNG
© 1994 PAWS, INC./Distributed by Universal Press Syndicate
RIIINNNG
FLUSH
RIIINNNNNNN
NNBLUB
NBLUB
NBLUB
NBLUB
JIM DAVIS
10-2
THE TOILET IS RINGING! WHAT SHOULD I DO?
RINNGG
TAKE A MESSAGE

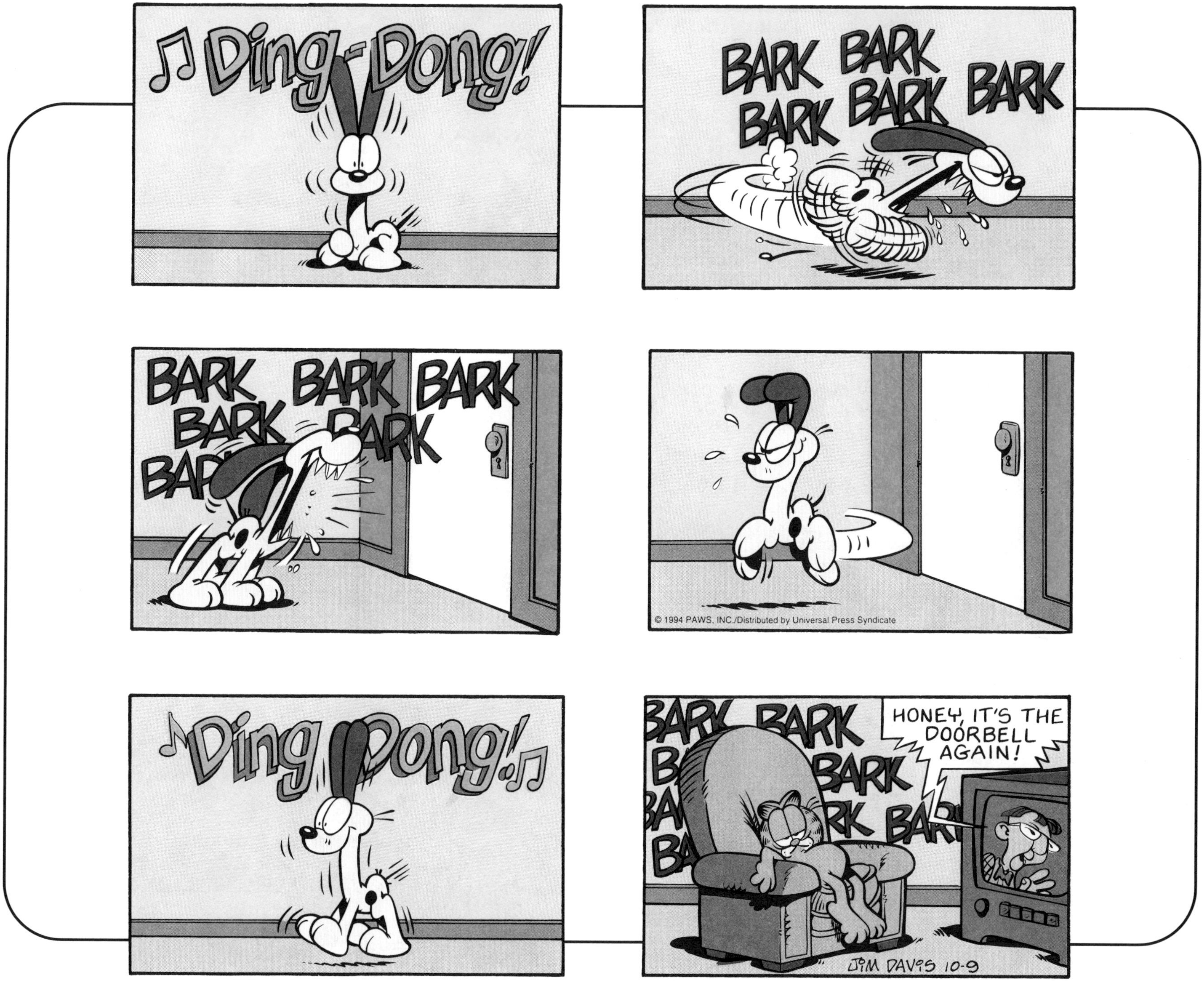
Ding-Dong!
BARK BARK BARK BARK BARK
BARK BARK BARK BARK BARK
Ding Dong!
BARK BARK BARK
HONEY, IT'S THE DOORBELL AGAIN!
JIM DAVIS 10-9

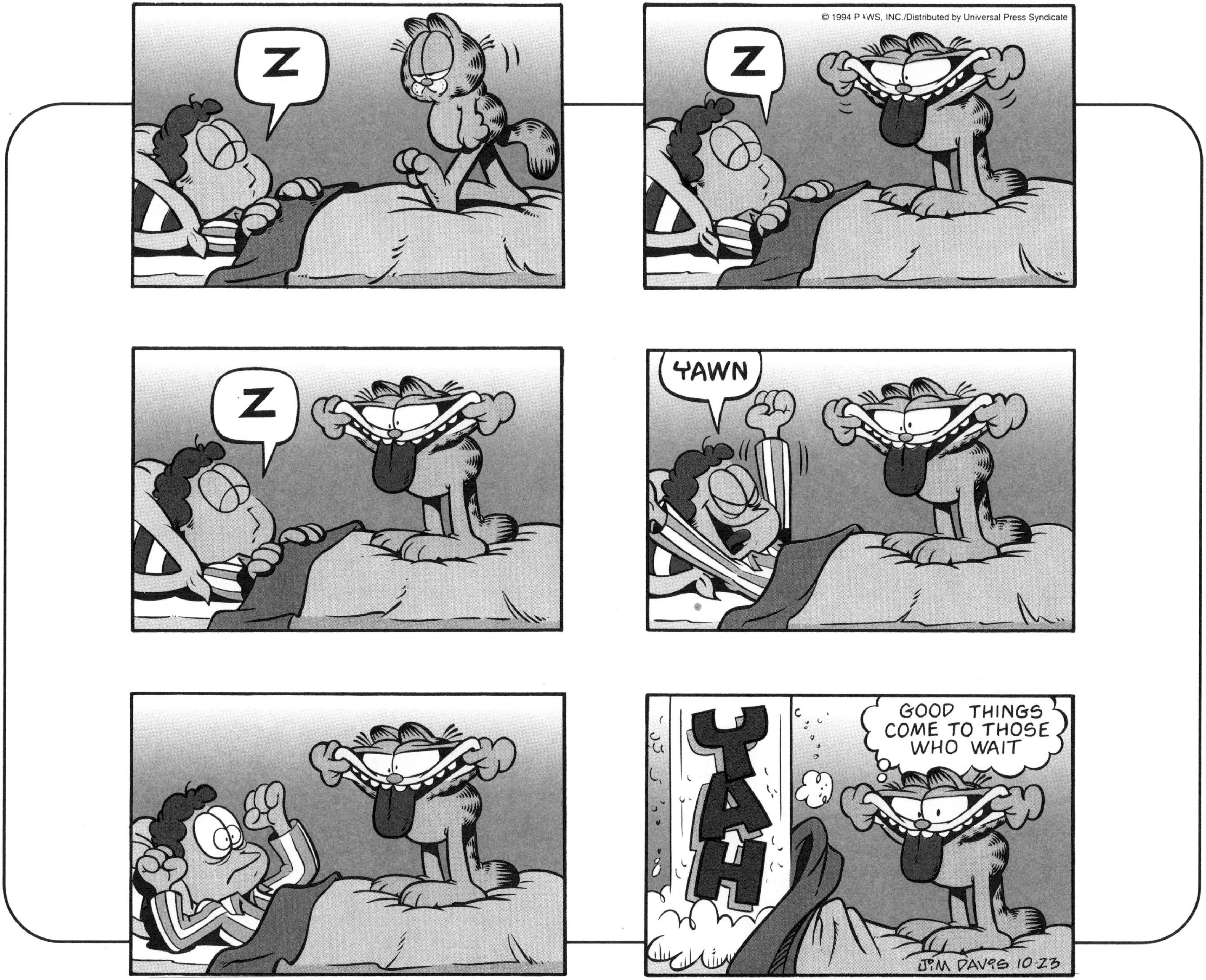
© 1994 PAWS, INC./Distributed by Universal Press Syndicate
Z
Z
Z
YAWN
YAH
GOOD THINGS COME TO THOSE WHO WAIT
JIM DAVIS 10-23

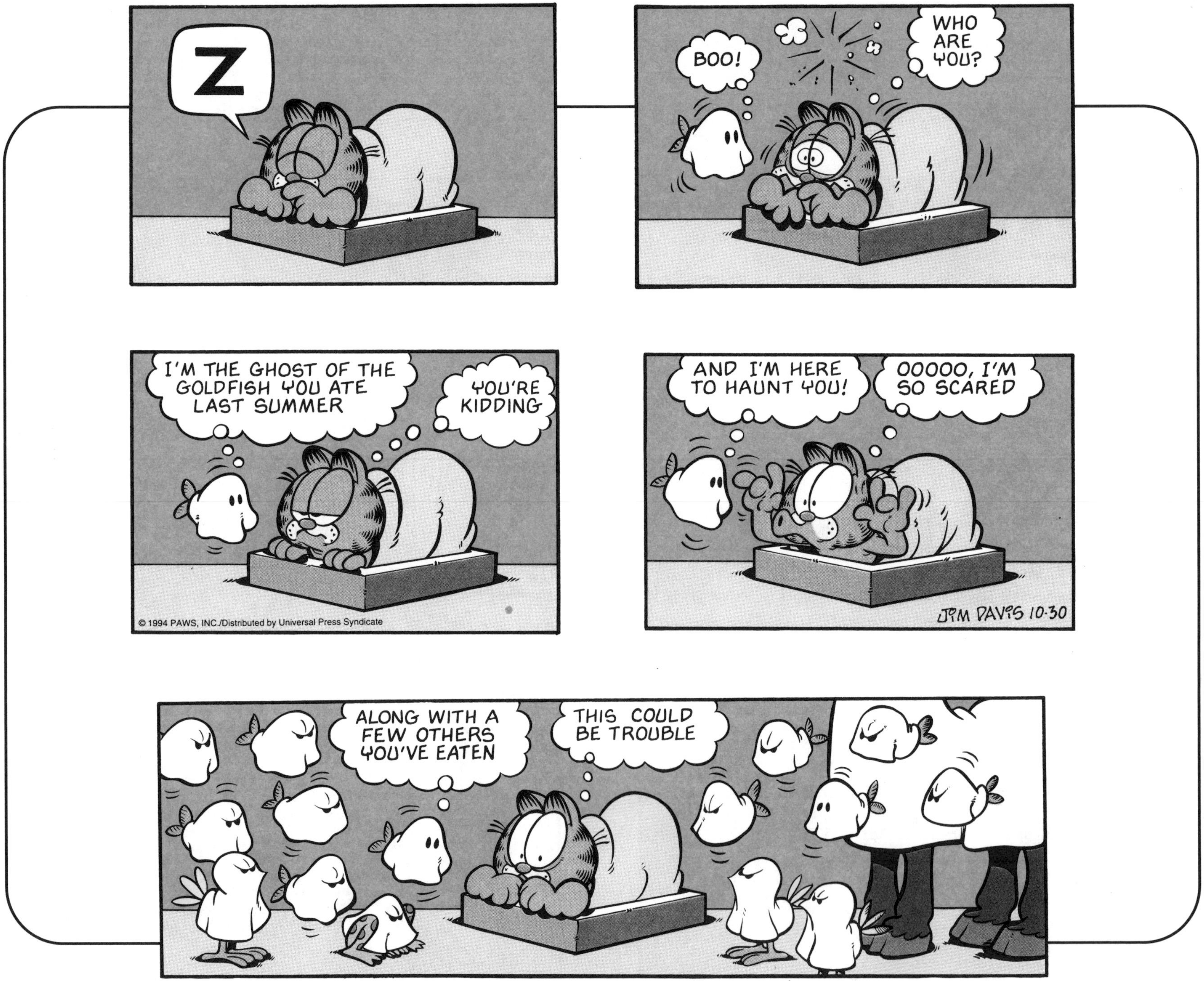
Z
BOO!
WHO ARE YOU?
I'M THE GHOST OF THE GOLDFISH YOU ATE LAST SUMMER
YOU'RE KIDDING
AND I'M HERE TO HAUNT YOU!
OOOOO, I'M SO SCARED
© 1994 PAWS, INC./Distributed by Universal Press Syndicate
JIM DAVIS 10-30
ALONG WITH A FEW OTHERS YOU'VE EATEN
THIS COULD BE TROUBLE

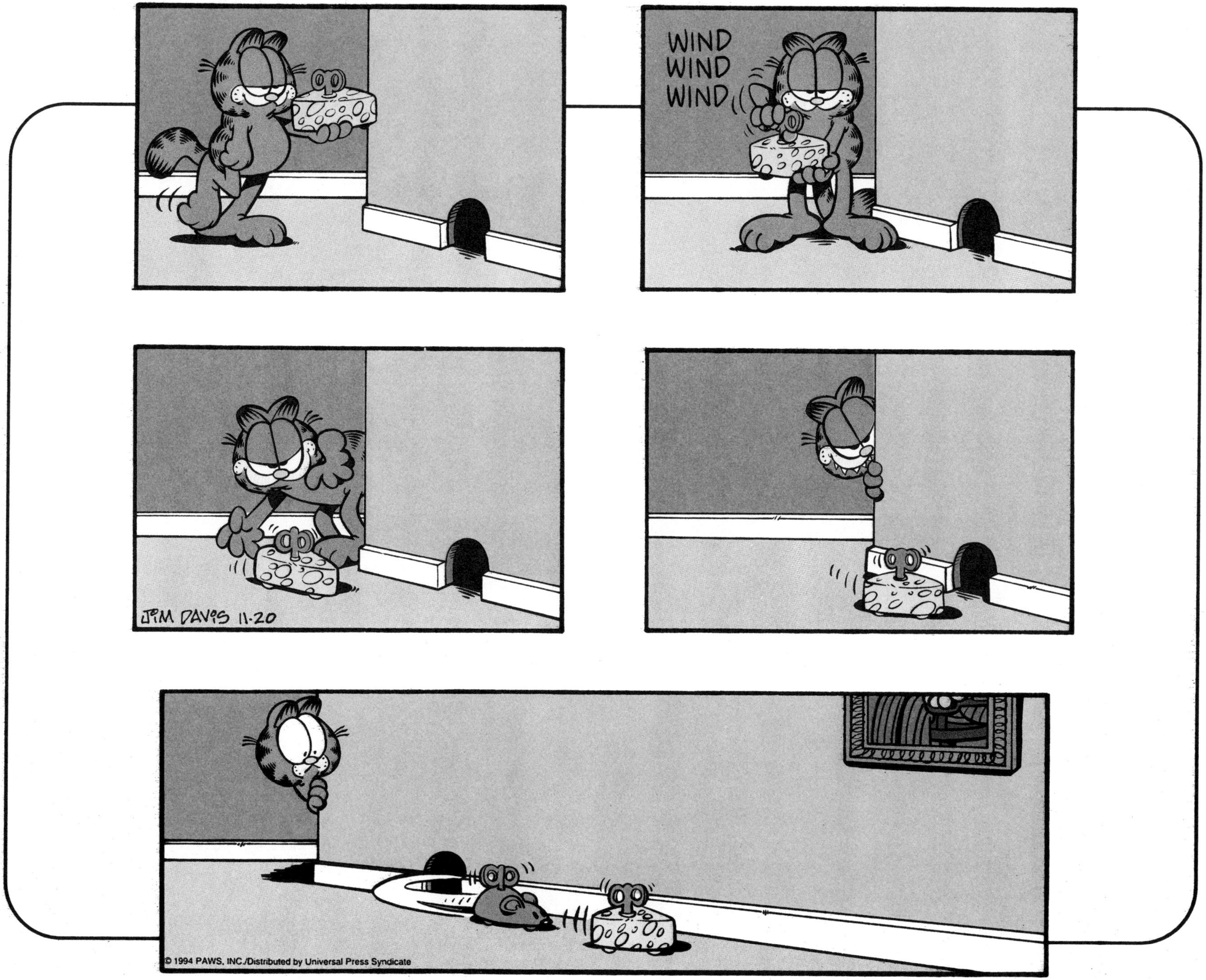
WIND
WIND
WIND
JIM DAVIS 11-20
© 1994 PAWS, INC./Distributed by Universal Press Syndicate

SHOOP!

GULP!

JIM DAVIS 11-27

© 1994 PAWS, INC./Distributed by Universal Press Syndicate

JiM DAViS 12-4

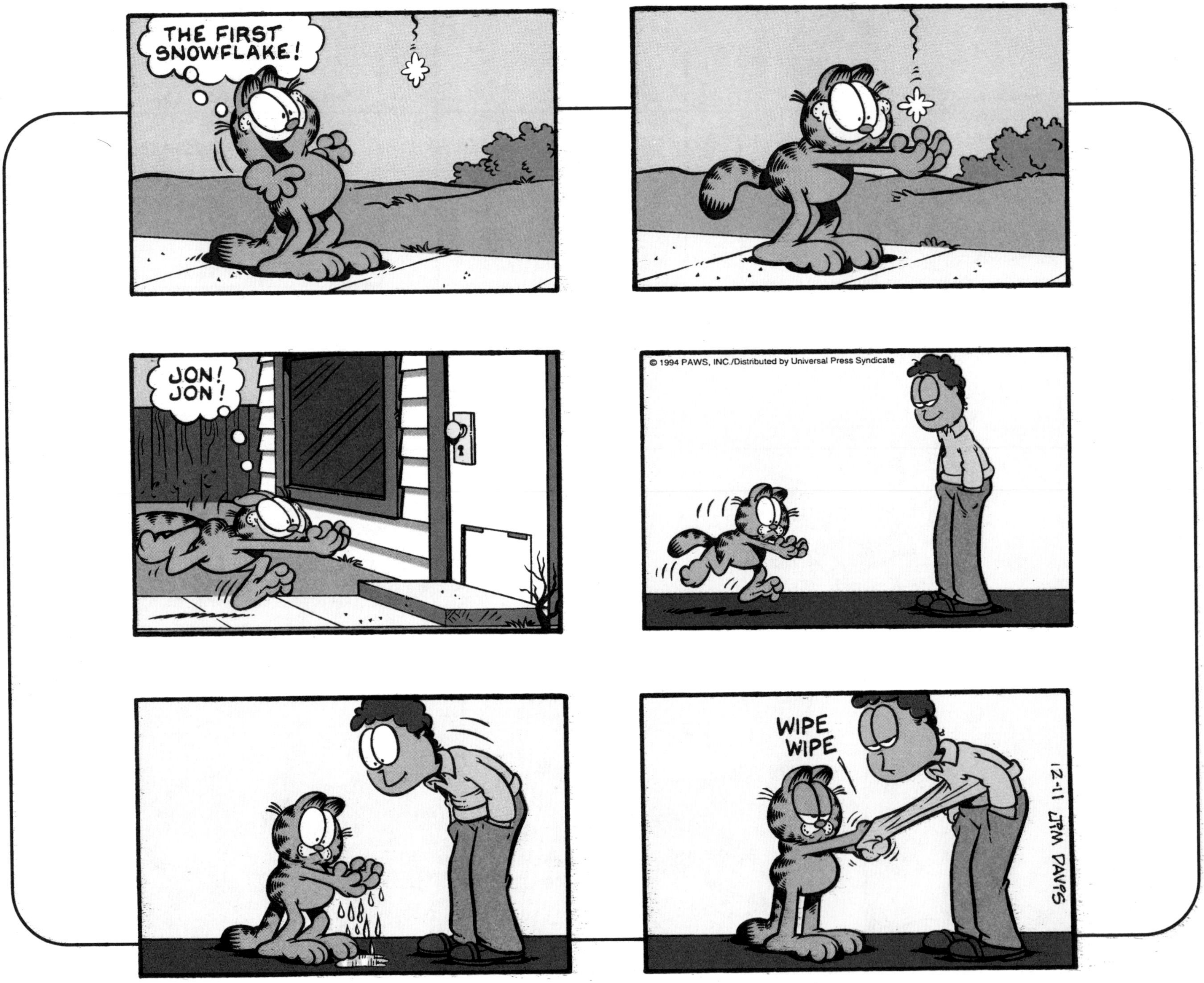
THE FIRST SNOWFLAKE!
JON! JON!
© 1994 PAWS, INC./Distributed by Universal Press Syndicate
WIPE WIPE
12-11 JPM DAVIS

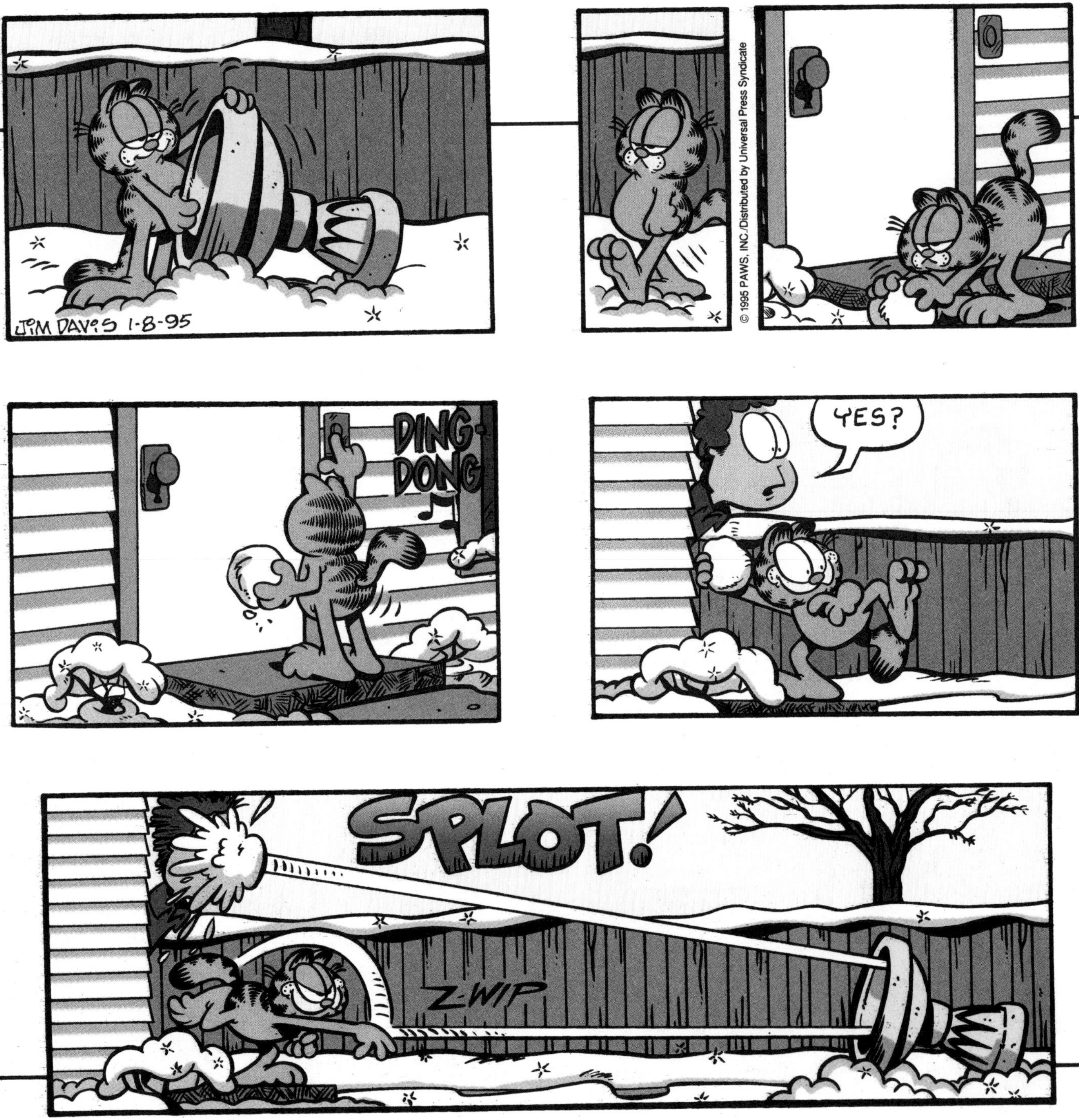
JIM DAVIS 1-8-95
© 1995 PAWS, INC./Distributed by Universal Press Syndicate
DING-DONG
YES?
SPLOT!
Z-WIP

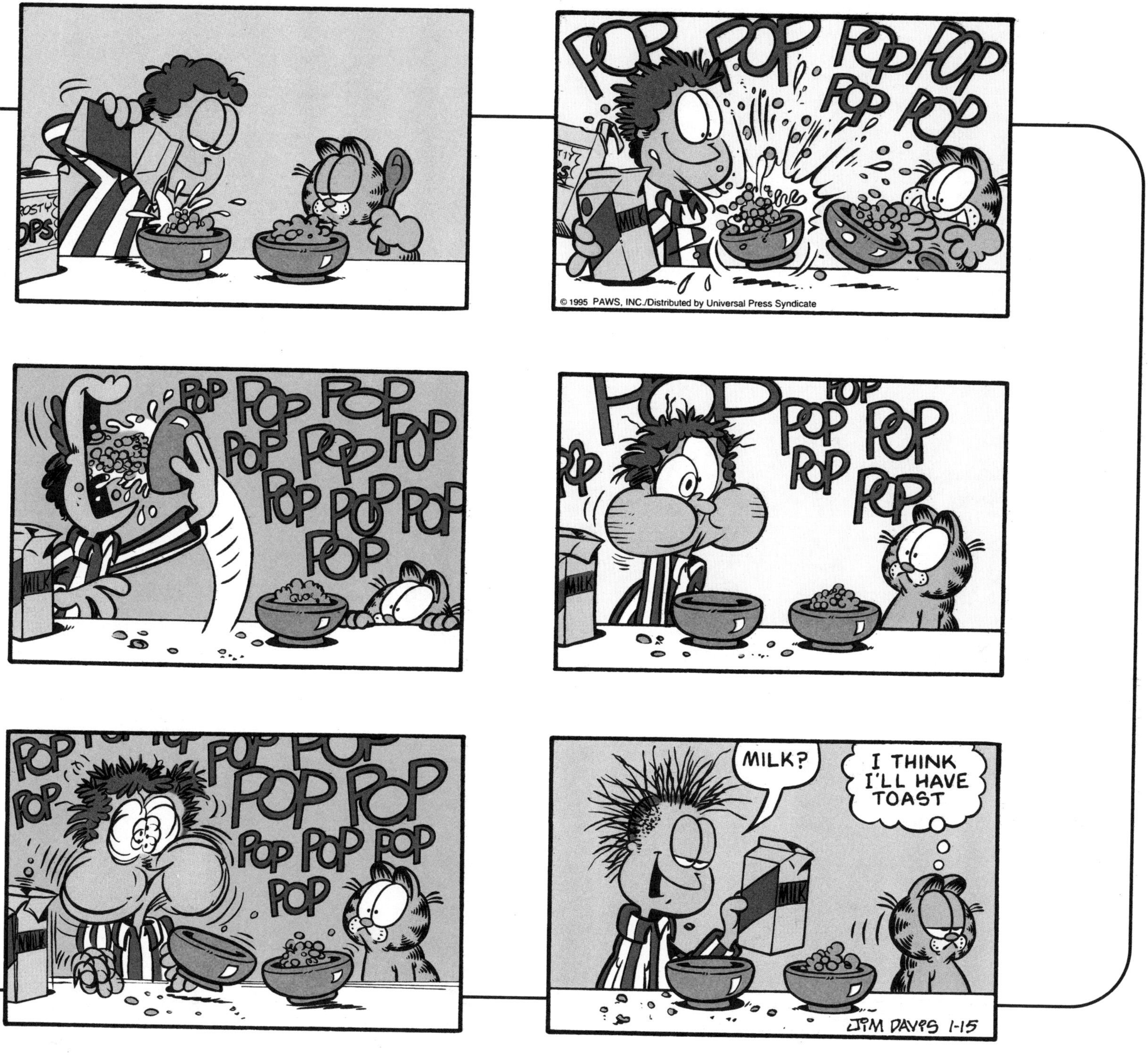
POP POP POP POP
POP POP
© 1995 PAWS, INC./Distributed by Universal Press Syndicate
MILK?
I THINK I'LL HAVE TOAST
JIM DAVIS 1-15

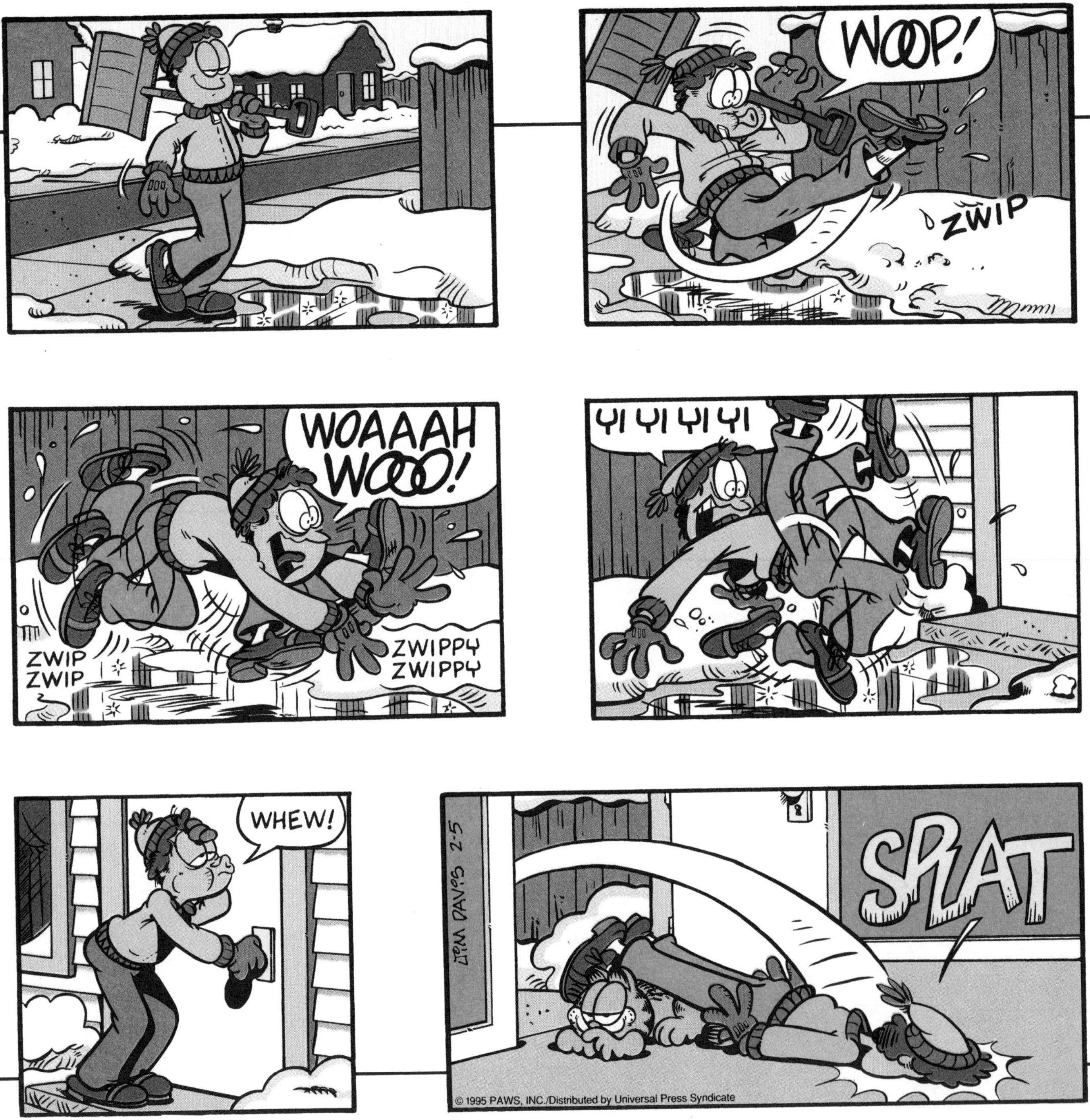
WOOP!
ZWIP
WOAAAH WOOO!
ZWIP ZWIP
ZWIPPY ZWIPPY
YI YI YI YI
WHEW!
JIM DAVIS 2-5
SPLAT

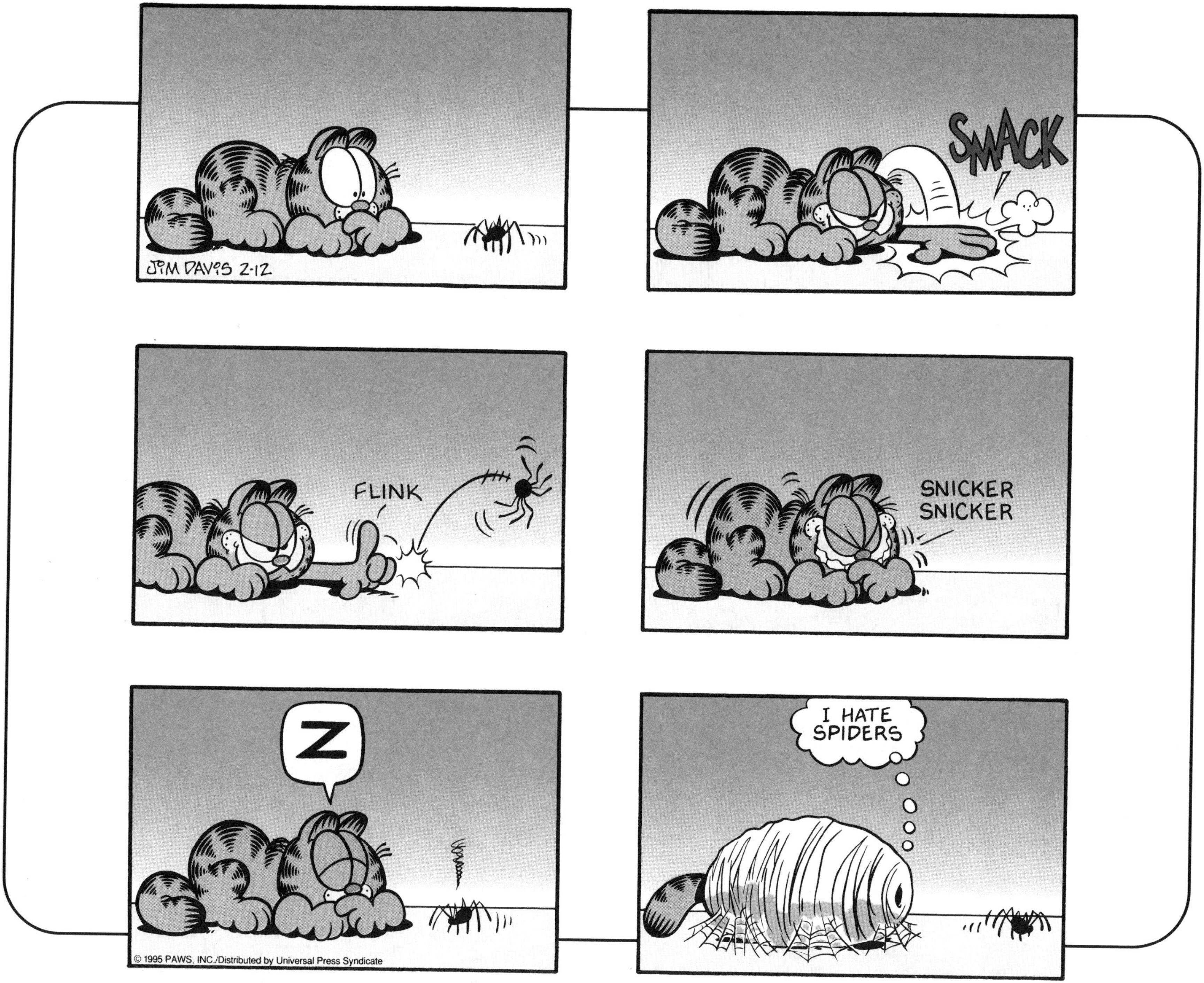
JIM DAVIS 2-12
SMACK
FLINK
SNICKER SNICKER
Z
I HATE SPIDERS
© 1995 PAWS, INC./Distributed by Universal Press Syndicate

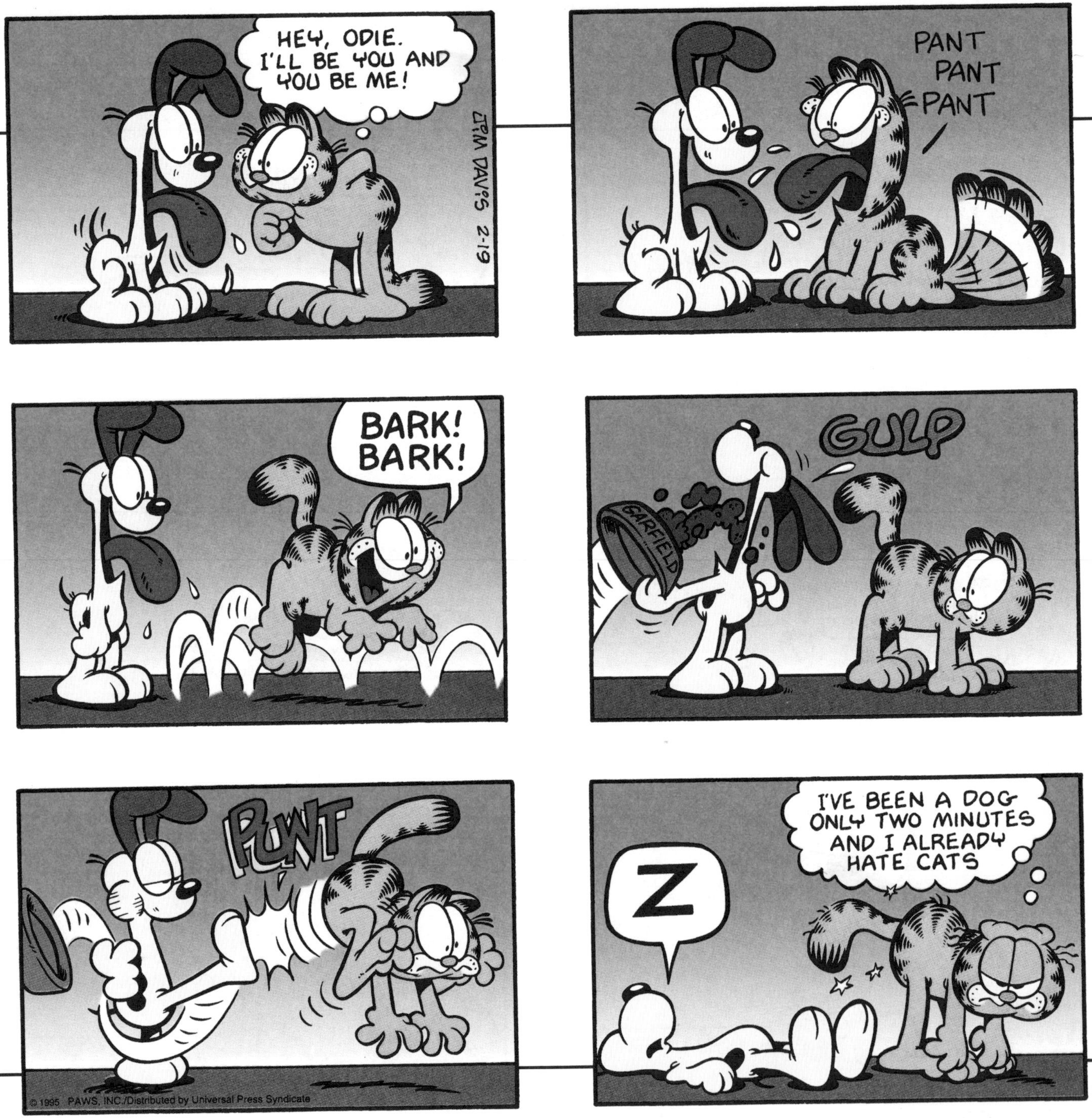

HEY, ODIE. I'LL BE YOU AND YOU BE ME!
JIM DAVIS 2-19
PANT PANT PANT
BARK! BARK!
GULP
GARFIELD
PUNT
Z
I'VE BEEN A DOG ONLY TWO MINUTES AND I ALREADY HATE CATS

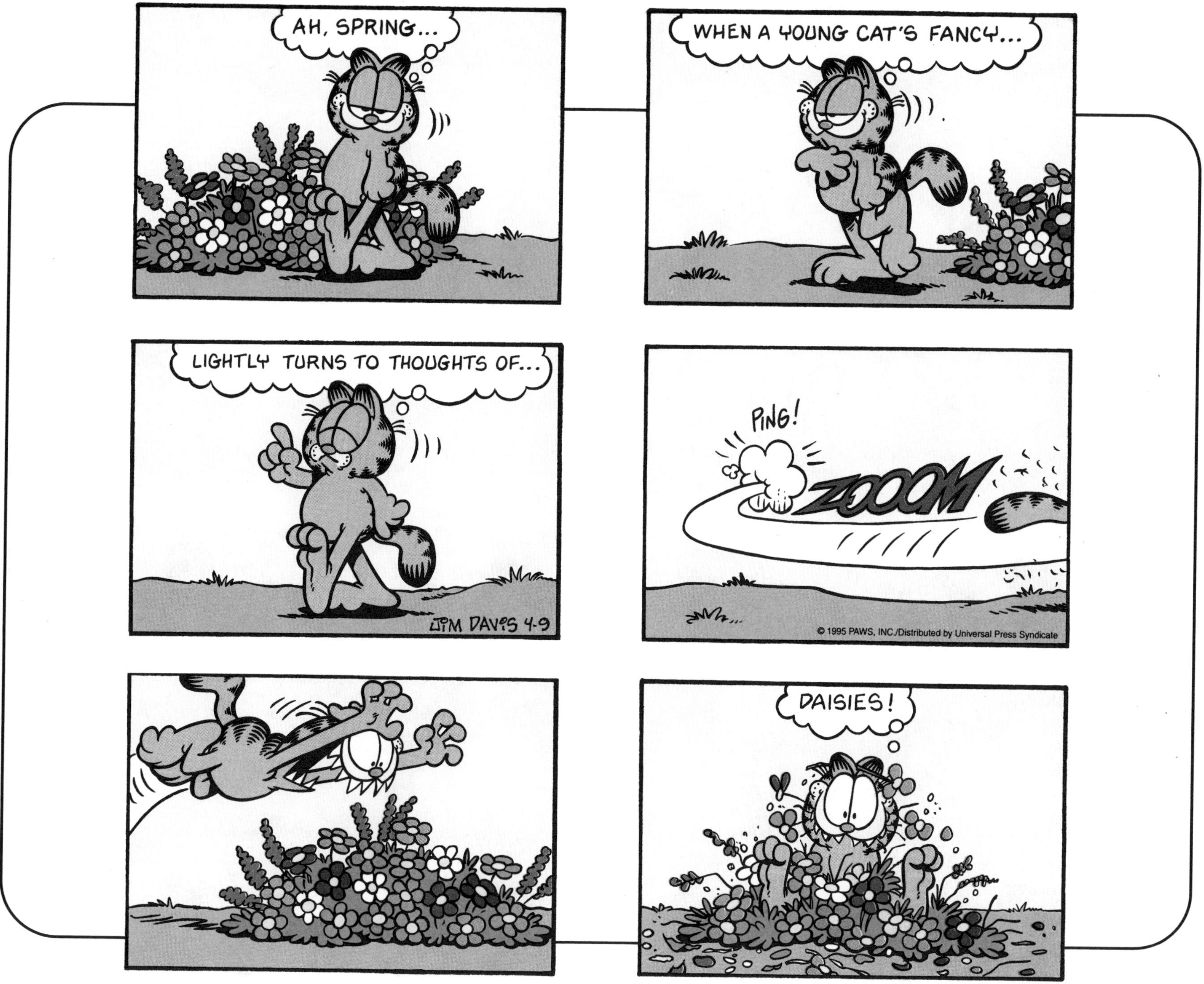
AH, SPRING...
WHEN A YOUNG CAT'S FANCY...
LIGHTLY TURNS TO THOUGHTS OF...
JIM DAVIS 4-9
PING!
ZOOOM
© 1995 PAWS, INC./Distributed by Universal Press Syndicate
DAISIES!

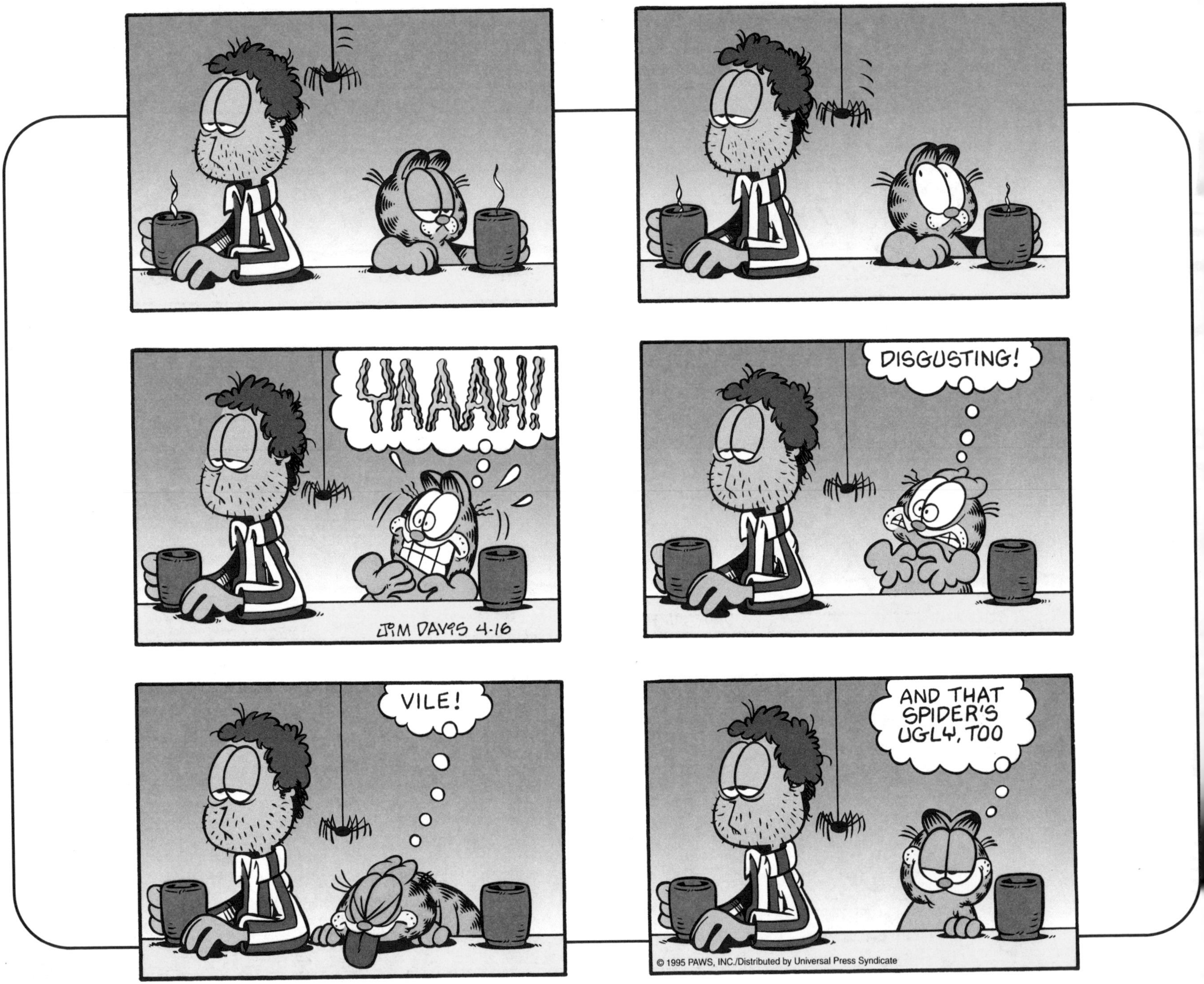
YAAAH!
JIM DAVIS 4-16
DISGUSTING!
VILE!
AND THAT SPIDER'S UGLY, TOO
© 1995 PAWS, INC./Distributed by Universal Press Syndicate

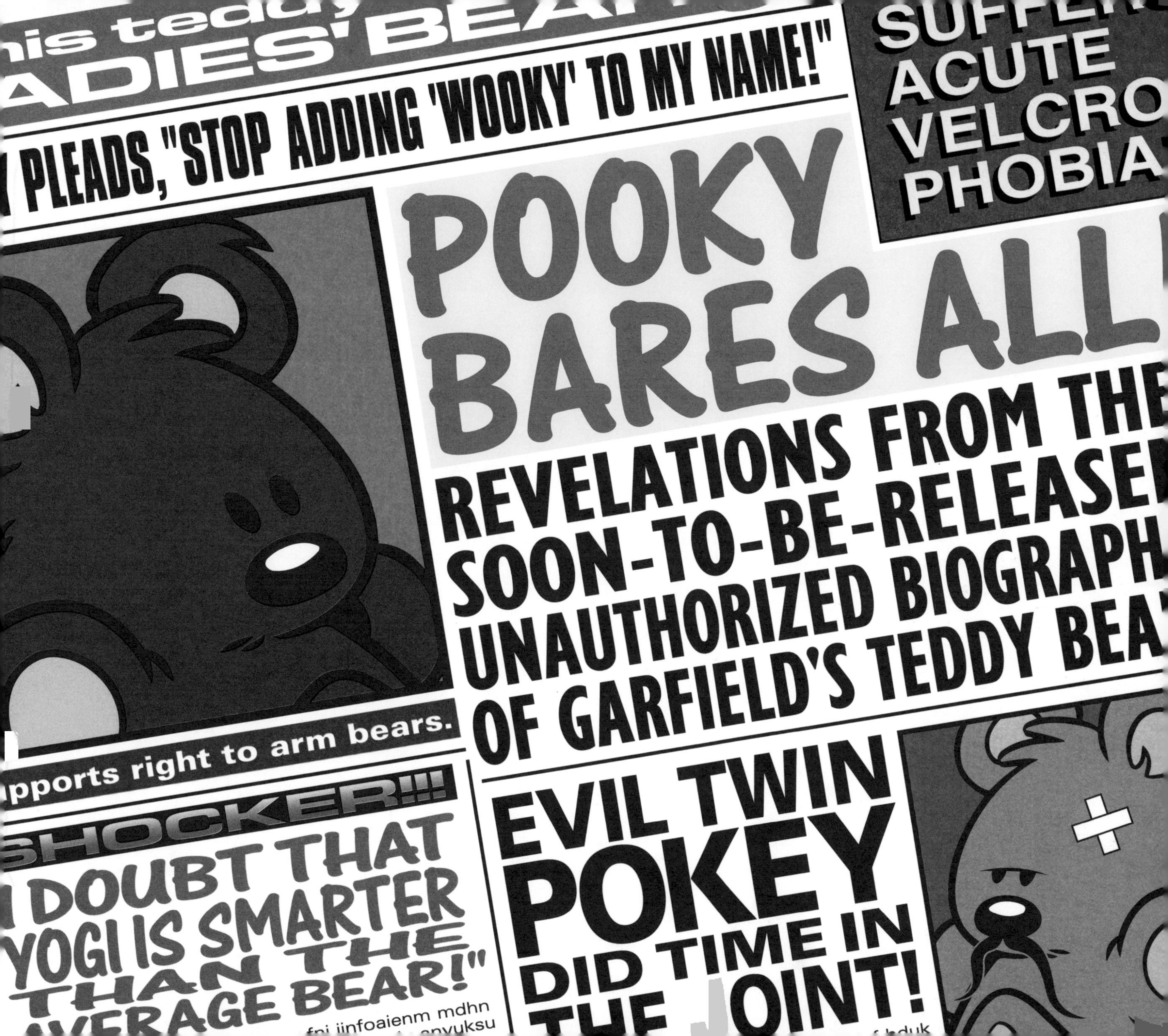

PLEADS, "STOP ADDING 'WOOKY' TO MY NAME!"
ACUTE
VELCRO
PHOBIA
POOKY BARES ALL
REVELATIONS FROM THE
SOON-TO-BE-RELEASE
UNAUTHORIZED BIOGRAPH
OF GARFIELD'S TEDDY BEA
pports right to arm bears.
SHOCKER!!!
DOUBT THAT
YOGI IS SMARTER
THAN THE
VERAGE BEAR!"
EVIL TWIN
POKEY
DID TIME IN
THE JOINT!